THE SMOKY G

And Other Inner Earth

THE SMOKY GOD

And Other Inner Earth Mysteries

Updated/Expanded Edition

Edited by Timothy Green Beckley

**Additional Material by Commander X,
Scott Corrales, Dennis Crenshaw,
Brad Steiger, Tim Swartz and Sean Casteel**

THE SMOKY GOD

AND OTHER INNER EARTH MYSTERIES

UPDATED/EXPANDED EDITION

ISBN: 1606111574
EAN: 9781606111574

Nonfiction

Timothy Green Beckley—Editorial Director
Carol Rodriquez—Publisher's Assistant
Sean Casteel—Associate Editor
Tim Swartz—Editorial Assistant
Typesetting, Formatting and Cover Design: William Kern

Printed in the United States of America

For a Free catalog, write:
Global Communications
P. O. Box 753
New Brunswick, NJ 08903
Free subscription to Conspiracy Journal e-mail Newsletter
www.ConspircayJournal.com

CONTENTS

Introduction by Timothy Green Beckley iv
Title Page And Dedication 1
Part One: Author's Foreword 2
Part Two: Olaf Jansen's Story 24
Part Three: Beyond the North Wind 47
Part Four: In the Under World 76
Part Five: Among the Ice Packs 94
Part Six: Conclusion 105
Part Seven: Author's Afterword 113
Part Eight: Saucers From Earth By Ray Palmer 116
Introduction
A Challenge to Secrecy
Part Nine: By The World Ascension Network 161
Secrets of the Subterranean Cities
The Agartha Network
Capitol Cities
Spotlight on Telos
Introducing the Woman from Telos, the City Beneath Mount Shasta—Sharula
Part Ten: By Commander X 187
Aliens & Atlanteans of Mount Shasta
The Girl From Beneath Mt. Shasta
Travel To The Center Of The Earth And Find It Teeming With Life! By Timothy Green Beckley 205
The Cosmic Battle Has Begun
Inner Earth People vs Outer Space Aliens
The Teachings Of Rev. William L. Blessing 209
Deep Underground By Scott Corrales 221
In Search Of Dark Realms
Underground Empires By Scott Corrales 240
Fact Or Fiction?
Why Were The Nazi War Machine And The U. S. Waging An All Out Battle To Get To The Poles First? By Dennis Crenshaw 267
Dr. Brooks Agnew By Tim Swartz 287
The Elder Ones from the Inner Earth By Brad Steiger 307
The Hollow Earth Hassle Of Mary Jane Martin And The Incredible Story Of Richard Shaver By Sean Casteel 327

Introduction

by Timothy Green Beckley

Over the years, there has been a proven fascination with what may lay within the core of our own planet.

More than a hundred years ago, the famous science fiction writer Jules Verne wowed us with an eerie tale entitled ***Journey to the Center of the Earth*** (which was made into a Hollywood movie starring, of all people, Pat Boone). Though most of us would consider this work to be more of a novel than actual reality, the truth of the matter is indeed quite a bit more startling.

Around the same time that Verne's creation was originally published, there was a strong belief among many that our planet was actually hollow and populated by a race of super beings. Many decades later, Hitler saw these entities as being part of an advanced "Aryan Race" whom he hoped to communicate with.

Less known is a very rare manuscript that has been privately circulated for many years among metaphysical students, ***The Smoky God***, which is presented as the true story of an individual who actually sailed into the Inner Earth and was befriended by giants the likes of whom have not walked on the outside of our planet since early Biblical times.

Now, Inner Light Publications is honored to present not only this rarely seen and long out of print manuscript, but also a totally new and valuable reference book that sheds great light on what has often been presented as a very dark and "shadowy" subject

Here at last is evidence that we do not have to look towards outer space for the origin of all UFOs, but that some "space ships" may be coming from a lot closer to home.

Read—Enjoy—Learn.

Tim Beckley, New Brunswick, NJ

THE SMOKY GOD

OR

A Voyage to the Inner World

By

Willis George Emerson

Dedicated To MY Chum And Companion
Bonnie Emerson My Wife

CONTENTS

PART I. AUTHOR'S FOREWORD

PART II. OLAF JANSEN'S STORY

PART III. BEYOND THE NORTH WIND

PART IV. IN THE UNDER WORLD

PART V. AMONG THE ICE PACKS

PART VI. CONCLUSION

PART VII. AUTHOR'S AFTERWORD

The Smoky God

Or A Voyage to the Inner World

"He is the God who sits in the center, on the navel of the earth, and he is the interpreter of religion to all mankind." — PLATO.

PART ONE

AUTHOR'S FOREWORD

I FEAR the seemingly incredible story which I am about to relate will be regarded as the result of a distorted intellect superinduced, possibly, by the glamour of unveiling a marvelous mystery, rather than a truthful record of the unparalleled experiences related by one Olaf Jansen, whose eloquent madness so appealed to my imagination that all thought of an analytical criticism has been effectually dispelled.

Marco Polo will doubtless shift uneasily in his grave at the strange story I am called upon to chronicle; a story as strange as a Munchausen tale. It is also incongruous that I, a disbeliever, should be the one to edit the story of Olaf Jansen, whose name is now for the first time given to the world, yet who must hereafter rank as one of the notables of earth.

I freely confess his statements admit of no rational analysis, but have to do with the profound mystery concerning the frozen North that for centuries has claimed the attention of scientists and laymen alike.

However much they are at variance with the cosmographical manuscripts of the past, these plain statements may be relied upon as a record of the things Olaf Jansen claims to have seen with his own eyes.

A hundred times I have asked myself

whether it is possible that the world's geography is incomplete, and that the startling narrative of Olaf Jansen is predicated upon demonstrable facts. The reader may be able to answer these queries to his own satisfaction, however far the chronicler of this narrative may be from having reached a conviction. Yet sometimes even I am at a loss to know whether I have been led away from an abstract truth by the ignes fatui of a clever superstition, or whether heretofore accepted facts are, after all, founded upon falsity.

It may be that the true home of Apollo was not at Delphi, but in that older earth-center of which Plato speaks, where he says: "Apollo's real home is among the Hyperboreans, in a land of perpetual life, where mythology tells us two doves flying from the two opposite ends of the world met in this fair region, the home of Apollo. Indeed, according to Hecataeus, Leto, the mother of Apollo, was born on an island in the Arctic Ocean far beyond the North Wind."

It is not my intention to attempt a discussion of the theogony of the deities nor the cosmogony of the world. My simple duty is to enlighten the world concerning a heretofore unknown portion of the universe, as it was seen and described by the old Norseman, Olaf Jansen.

Interest in northern research is international. Eleven nations are engaged in, or have contributed to, the perilous work of trying to solve Earth's one remaining cosmological mystery.

There is a saying, ancient as the hills, that "truth is stranger than fiction," and in a most startling manner has this axiom been brought home to me within the last fortnight.

It was just two o'clock in the morning when I was aroused from a restful sleep by the vigorous ringing of my door-bell. The untimely disturber proved to be a messenger bearing a note, scrawled almost to the point of illegibility, from an old Norseman by the name of Olaf Jansen. After much deciphering, I made out the writing, which simply said: "Am ill unto death. Come." The call was imperative, and I lost no time in making ready to comply.

Perhaps I may as well explain here that Olaf Jansen, a man who quite recently celebrated his ninety-fifth birthday, has for the last half-dozen years been living alone in an unpretentious bungalow out Glendale way, a short distance from the business district of Los Angeles, California.

It was less than two years ago, while out walking one afternoon that I was attracted by Olaf Jansen's house and its homelike surroundings, toward its owner and occupant, whom I afterward came to know as a believer in the ancient worship of Odin and Thor.

There was a gentleness in his face, and a kindly expression in the keenly alert gray eyes of this man who had lived more than four-score years and ten; and, withal, a sense of loneliness that appealed to my sympathy. Slightly stooped, and with his hands clasped behind him, he walked back and forth with slow and measured tread, that day when first we met. I can hardly say what particular motive impelled me to pause in my walk and engage him in conversation. He seemed pleased when I complimented him on the attractiveness of his bungalow, and on the well-tended vines and flowers clustering in profusion over its windows, roof and wide piazza.

I soon discovered that my new acquaintance was no ordinary person, but one profound and learned to a remarkable degree; a man who, in the later years of his long life, had dug deeply into books and become strong in the power of meditative silence.

I encouraged him to talk, and soon gathered that he had resided only six or seven years in Southern California, but had passed the dozen years prior in one of the middle Eastern states. Before that he had been a fisherman off the coast of Norway, in the region of the Lofoden Islands, from whence he had made trips still farther north to Spitzbergen and even to Franz Josef Land.

When I started to take my leave, he seemed reluctant to have me go, and asked me to come again. Although at the time I thought nothing of it, I remember now that he made a peculiar remark as I extended my hand in leave-taking. "You will come again?" he asked. "Yes, you will come again some day. I am sure you will; and I shall show you my library and tell you many things of which you have never dreamed, things so wonderful that it may be you will not believe me."

I laughingly assured him that I would not only come again, but would be ready to believe whatever he might choose to tell me of his travels and adventures.

In the days that followed I became well acquainted with Olaf Jansen, and, little by little, he told me his story, so marvelous, that its very daring challenges reason and belief. The old Norseman always expressed himself with so much earnestness and sincerity that I became enthralled by his strange narrations.

Then came the messenger's call that night, and within the hour I was at Olaf Jansen's bungalow.

He was very impatient at the long wait, although after being summoned I had come immediately to his bedside.

"I must hasten," he exclaimed, while yet he held my hand in greeting. "I have much to tell you that you know not, and I will trust no one but you. I fully realize," he went on hurriedly, "that I shall not survive the night. The time has come to join my fathers in the great sleep."

I adjusted the pillows to make him more comfortable, and assured him I was glad to be able to serve him in any way possible, for I was beginning to realize the seriousness of his condition.

The lateness of the hour, the stillness of the surroundings, the uncanny feeling of being alone with the dying man, together with his weird story, all combined to make my heart beat fast and loud with a feeling for which I have no name. Indeed, there were many times that night by the old Norseman's couch, and there have been many times since, when a sensation rather than a conviction took possession of my very soul, and I seemed not only to believe in, but actually see, the strange lands, the strange people and the strange world of which he told, and to hear the mighty orchestral chorus of a thousand lusty voices.

For over two hours he seemed endowed with almost superhuman strength, talking rapidly, and to all appearances, rationally. Finally he gave into my hands certain data, drawings and crude maps. "These," said he in conclusion, "I leave in your hands. If I can have your promise to give them to the world, I shall die happy, because I desire that people may know the truth, for then all mystery concerning the frozen Northland will be explained. There is no chance of your suffering the fate I suffered. They will not put you in irons, nor confine you in a mad-house, because you are not telling your own story, but mine, and I, thanks to the gods, Odin and Thor, will be in my grave, and so beyond the reach of disbelievers who would persecute."

Without a thought of the farreaching results the promise entailed, or foreseeing the many sleepless nights which the obligation has since brought me, I gave my hand and with it a pledge to discharge faithfully his dying wish.

As the sun rose over the peaks of the San

Jacinto, far to the eastward, the spirit of Olaf Jansen, the navigator, the explorer and worshiper of Odin and Thor, the man whose experiences and travels, as related, are without a parallel in all the world's history, passed away, and I was left alone with the dead.

And now, after having paid the last sad rites to this strange man from the Lofoden Islands, and the still farther "Northward Ho!", the courageous explorer of frozen regions, who in his declining years (after he had passed the four-score mark) had sought an asylum of restful peace in sun-favored California, I will undertake to make public his story.

But, first of all, let me indulge in one or two reflections:

Generation follows generation, and the traditions from the misty past are handed down from sire to son, but for some strange reason interest in the ice-locked unknown does not abate with the receding years, either in the minds of the ignorant or the tutored.

With each new generation a restless impulse stirs the hearts of men to capture the veiled citadel of the Arctic, the circle of silence, the land of glaciers, cold wastes of waters and winds that are strangely warm. Increasing interest is manifested in the mountainous icebergs, and marvelous speculations are indulged in concerning the earth's center of gravity, the cradle of the tides, where the whales have their nurseries, where the magnetic needle goes mad, where the Aurora Borealis illumines the night, and where brave and courageous spirits of every generation dare to venture and explore, defying the dangers of the "Farthest North."

One of the ablest works of recent years is ***"Paradise Found, or the Cradle of The Human Race at the North Pole,"*** by William F. Warren. In his carefully prepared volume, Mr. Warren almost stubbed his toe against the real truth, but missed it seemingly by only a hair's breadth, if the old Norseman's revelation be true.

Dr. Orville Livingston Leech, scientist, in a recent article, says:

"The possibilities of a land inside the earth were first brought to my attention when I picked up a geode on the shores of the Great Lakes. The geode is a spherical and apparently solid stone, but when broken is found to be hollow and coated with crystals. The earth is only a larger form of a geode, and the law that created the geode in its hollow form undoubtedly fashioned the earth in the same way."

In presenting the theme of this almost incredible story, as told by Olaf Jansen, and supplemented by manuscript, maps and crude drawings entrusted to me, a fitting introduction is found in the following quotation:

"In the beginning God created the heaven and the earth, and the earth was without form and void." And also, "God created man in his own image." Therefore, even in things material, man must be God-like, because he is created in the likeness of the Father.

A man builds a house for himself and family. The porches or verandas are all without, and are secondary. The building is really constructed for the conveniences within.

Olaf Jansen makes the startling announcement through me, an humble instrument, that in like manner, God created the earth for the "within" — that is to say, for its lands, seas, rivers, mountains, forests and valleys, and for its other internal conveniences, while the outside surface of the earth is merely the veranda, the porch, where things grow by comparison but sparsely, like the lichen on the mountain side, clinging determinedly for bare existence.

Take an egg-shell, and from each end break out a piece as large as the end of this pencil. Extract its contents, and then you will have a perfect representation of Olaf Jansen's earth. The distance from the inside surface to the outside surface, according to him, is about three hundred miles. The center of gravity is not in the center of the earth, but in the center of the shell or crust; therefore, if the thickness of the earth's crust or shell is three hundred miles, the center of gravity is one hundred and fifty miles below the surface.

In their log-books Arctic explorers tell us of the dipping of the needle as the vessel sails in regions of the farthest north known. In reality, they are at the curve; on the edge of the shell, where gravity is geometrically increased, and while the electric current seemingly dashes off into space toward the phantom idea of the North Pole, yet this same electric current drops again and continues its course southward along the inside surface of the earth's crust.

In the appendix to his work, Captain Sabine gives an account of experiments to determine the acceleration of the pendulum in different latitudes. This appears to have resulted from the joint labor of Peary and Sabine. He says: "The accidental discovery that a pendulum on being removed from Paris to the neighborhood of the equator increased its time of vibration, gave the first step to our present knowledge that the polar axis of the globe is less than the equatorial; that the force of gravity at the surface of the earth increases progressively from the equator toward the poles."

According to Olaf Jansen, in the beginning this old world of ours was created solely for the "within" world, where are located the four great rivers — the Euphrates, the Pison, the Gihon and the Hiddekel. These same names of rivers, when applied to streams on the "outside" surface of the earth, are purely traditional from an antiquity beyond the memory of man.

On the top of a high mountain, near the fountain-head of these four rivers, Olaf Jansen, the Norseman, claims to have discovered the long-lost "Garden of Eden," the veritable navel of the earth, and to have spent over two years studying and reconnoitering in this marvelous "within" land, exuberant with stupendous plant life and abounding in giant animals; a land where the people live to be centuries old, after the order of Methuselah and other Biblical characters; a region where one-quarter of the "inner" surface is water and three-quarters land; where there are large oceans and many rivers and lakes; where the cities are superlative in construction and magnificence; where modes of transportation are as far in advance of ours as we with our boasted achievements are in advance of the inhabitants of "darkest Africa."

The distance directly across the space from inner surface to inner surface is about six hundred miles less than the recognized diameter of the earth. In the identical center of this vast vacuum is the seat of electricity — a mammoth ball of dull red fire — not startlingly brilliant, but surrounded by a white, mild, luminous cloud, giving out uniform warmth, and held in its place in the center of this internal space by the immutable law of gravitation. This electrical cloud is known to the people "within" as the abode of "The Smoky God." They believe it to be the throne of "The Most High."

Olaf Jansen reminded me of how, in the old college days, we were all familiar with the laboratory demonstrations of centrifugal motion, which clearly proved that, if the earth were a solid, the rapidity of its revolution upon its axis would tear it into a thousand fragments.

The old Norseman also maintained that from the farthest points of land on the islands of Spitzbergen and Franz Josef Land, flocks of geese may be seen annually flying still farther northward, just as the sailors and explorers record in their logbooks. No scientist has yet been audacious enough to attempt to explain, even to his own satisfaction, toward what lands these winged fowls are guided by their subtle instinct. However, Olaf Jansen has given us a most reasonable explanation.

The presence of the open sea in the Northland is also explained. Olaf Jansen claims that the northern aperture, intake or hole, so to speak, is about fourteen hundred miles across. In connection with this, let us read what Explorer Nansen writes, on page 288 of his book: "I have never had such a splendid sail. On to the north, steadily north, with a good wind, as fast as steam and sail can take us, an open sea mile after mile, watch after watch, through these unknown regions, always clearer and clearer of ice, one might almost say: 'How long will it last?' The eye always turns to the northward as one paces the bridge. It is gazing into the future. But there is always the same dark sky ahead which means open sea." Again, the Norwood Review of England, in its issue of May 10, 1884, says: "We do not admit that there is ice up to the Pole — once inside the great ice barrier, a new world breaks upon the explorer, the climate is mild like that of England, and, afterward, balmy as the Greek Isles."

Some of the rivers "within," Olaf Jansen claims, are larger than our Mississippi and Amazon rivers combined, in point of volume of water carried; indeed their greatness is occasioned by their width and depth rather than their length, and it is at the mouths of these mighty rivers, as they flow northward and southward along the inside surface of the earth, that mammoth icebergs are found, some of them fifteen and twenty miles wide and from forty to one hundred miles in length.

Is it not strange that there has never been an iceberg encountered either in the Arctic or Antarctic Ocean that is not composed of fresh water? Modern scientists claim that freezing eliminates the salt, but Olaf Jansen claims differently.

Ancient Hindoo, Japanese and Chinese writings, as well as the hieroglyphics of the extinct races of the North American continent, all speak of the custom of sun-worshiping, and it is possible, in the startling light of Olaf Jansen's revelations, that the people of the inner world, lured away by glimpses of the sun as it shone upon the inner surface of the earth, either from the northern or the southern opening, became dissatisfied with "The Smoky God," the great pillar or mother cloud of electricity, and, weary of their continuously mild and pleasant atmosphere, followed the brighter light, and were finally led beyond the ice belt and scattered over the "outer" surface of the earth, through Asia, Europe, North America and, later, Africa, Australia and South America. [1]

[1 The following quotation is significant; "It follows that man issuing from a mother-region still undetermined but which a number of considerations indicate to have been in the North, has radiated in several directions; that his migrations have been constantly from North to South." — M. le Marquis G. de Saporta, in Popular Science Monthly, October, 1883, page 753.]

It is a notable fact that, as we approach the Equator, the stature of the human race grows less. But the Patagonians of South America are probably the only aborigines from the center of the earth who came out through the aperture usually designated as the South Pole, and they are called the giant race.

Olaf Jansen avers that, in the beginning, the world was created by the Great Architect of the Universe, so that man might dwell upon its "inside" surface, which has ever since been the habitation of the "chosen."

They who were driven out of the "Garden of Eden" brought their traditional history with them.

The history of the people living "within" contains a narrative suggesting the story of Noah and the ark with which we are familiar. He sailed away, as did Columbus, from a certain port, to a strange land he had heard of far to the northward, carrying with him all manner of beasts of the fields and fowls of the air, but was never heard of afterward.

On the northern boundaries of Alaska, and still more frequently on the Siberian coast, are found boneyards containing tusks of ivory in quantities so great as to suggest the burying-places of antiquity. From Olaf Jansen's account, they have come from the great prolific animal life that abounds in the fields and forests and on the banks of numerous rivers of the Inner World. The materials were caught in the ocean currents, or were carried on ice-floes, and have accumulated like driftwood on the Siberian coast. This has been going on for ages, and hence these mysterious bone-yards.

On this subject William F. Warren, in his book already cited, pages 297 and 298, says: "The Arctic rocks tell of a lost Atlantis more wonderful than Plato's. The fossil ivory beds of Siberia excel everything of the kind in the world. From the days of Pliny, at least, they have constantly been undergoing exploitation, and still they are the chief headquarters of supply. The remains of mammoths are so abundant that, as Gratacap says, 'the northern islands of Siberia seem built up of crowded bones.'

Another scientific writer, speaking of the islands of New Siberia, northward of the mouth of the River Lena, uses this language: 'Large quantities of ivory are dug out of the ground every year. Indeed, some of the islands are believed to be nothing but an accumulation of drift-timber and the bodies of mammoths and other antediluvian animals frozen together.' From this we may infer that, during the years that have elapsed since the Russian conquest of Siberia, useful tusks from more than twenty thousand mammoths have been collected."

But now for the story of Olaf Jansen. I give it in detail, as set down by himself in manuscript, and woven into the tale, just as he placed them, are certain quotations from recent works on Arctic exploration, showing how carefully the old Norseman compared with his own experiences those of other voyagers to the frozen North. Thus wrote the disciple of Odin and Thor:

PART TWO

OLAF JANSEN'S STORY

MY name is Olaf Jansen. I am a Norwegian, although I was born in the little seafaring Russian town of Uleaborg, on the eastern coast of the Gulf of Bothnia, the northern arm of the Baltic Sea.

My parents were on a fishing cruise in the Gulf of Bothnia, and put into this Russian town of Uleaborg at the time of my birth, being the twenty-seventh day of October, 1811.

My father, Jens Jansen, was born at Rodwig on the Scandinavian coast, near the Lofoden Islands, but after marrying made his home at Stockholm, because my mother's people resided in that city. When seven years old, I began going with my father on his fishing trips along the Scandinavian coast.

Early in life I displayed an aptitude for books, and at the age of nine years was placed in a private school in Stockholm, remaining there until I was fourteen. After this I made regular trips with my father on all his fishing voyages.

My father was a man fully six feet three in height, and weighed over fifteen stone, a typical Norseman of the most rugged sort, and capable of more endurance than any other man I have ever known. He possessed the gentleness of a woman in tender little ways, yet his determination and will-power were beyond description. His will admitted of no defeat.

I was in my nineteenth year when we started on what proved to be our last trip as fishermen, and which resulted in the strange story that shall be given to the world,— but not until I have finished my earthly pilgrimage.

I dare not allow the facts as I know them to be published while I am living, for fear of further humiliation, confinement and suffering. First of all, I was put in irons by the captain of the whaling vessel that rescued me, for no other reason than that I told the truth about the marvelous discoveries made by my father and myself. But this was far from being the end of my tortures.

After four years and eight months' absence I reached Stockholm, only to find my mother had died the previous year, and the property left by my parents in the possession of my mother's people, but it was at once made over to me.

All might have been well, had I erased from my memory the story of our adventure and of my father's terrible death.

Finally, one day I told the story in detail to my uncle, Gustaf Osterlind, a man of considerable property, and urged him to fit out an expedition for me to make another voyage to the strange land.

At first I thought he favored my project. He seemed interested, and invited me to go before certain officials and explain to them, as I had to him, the story of our travels and discoveries. Imagine my disappointment and horror when, upon the conclusion of my narrative, certain papers were signed by my uncle, and, without warning, I found myself arrested and hurried away to dismal and fearful confinement in a madhouse, where I remained for twenty-eight years — long, tedious, frightful years of suffering!

I never ceased to assert my sanity, and to protest against the injustice of my confinement. Finally, on the seventeenth of October, 1862, I was released. My uncle was dead, and the friends of my youth were now strangers. Indeed, a man over fifty years old, whose only known record is that of a madman, has no friends.

I was at a loss to know what to do for a living, but instinctively turned toward the harbor where fishing boats in great numbers were anchored, and within a week I had shipped with a fisherman by the name of Yan Hansen, who was starting on a long fishing cruise to the Lofoden Islands.

Here my earlier years of training proved of the very greatest advantage, especially in enabling me to make myself useful. This was but the beginning of other trips, and by frugal economy I was, in a few years, able to own a fishing-brig of my own. For twenty-seven years thereafter I followed the sea as a fisherman, five years working for others, and the last twenty-two for myself.

During all these years I was a most diligent student of books, as well as a hard worker at my business, but I took great care not to mention to anyone the story concerning the discoveries made by my father and myself. Even at this late day I would be fearful of having any one see or know the things I am writing, and the records and maps I have in my keeping. When my days on earth are finished, I shall leave maps and records that will enlighten and, I hope, benefit mankind.

The memory of my long confinement with maniacs, and all the horrible anguish and sufferings are too vivid to warrant my taking further chances.

In 1889 I sold out my fishing boats, and found I had accumulated a fortune quite sufficient to keep me the remainder of my life. I then came to America.

For a dozen years my home was in Illinois, near Batavia, where I gathered most of the books in my present library, though I brought many choice volumes from Stockholm. Later, I came to Los Angeles, arriving here March 4, 1901. The date I well remember, as it was President McKinley's second inauguration day. I bought this humble home and determined, here in the privacy of my own abode, sheltered by my own vine and fig-tree, and with my books about me, to make maps and drawings of the new lands we had discovered, and also to write the story in detail from the time my father and I left Stockholm until the tragic event that parted us in the Antarctic Ocean.

I well remember that we left Stockholm in our fishing-sloop on the third day of April, 1829, and sailed to the southward, leaving Gothland Island to the left and Oeland Island to the right. A few days later we succeeded in doubling Sandhommar Point, and made our way through the sound which separates Denmark from the Scandinavian coast. In due time we put in at the town of Christiansand, where we rested two days, and then started around the Scandinavian coast to the westward, bound for the Lofoden Islands.

My father was in high spirit, because of the excellent and gratifying returns he had received from our last catch by marketing at Stockholm, instead of selling at one of the seafaring towns along the Scandinavian coast. He was especially pleased with the sale of some ivory tusks that he had found on the west coast of Franz Joseph Land during one of his northern cruises the previous year, and he expressed the hope that this time we might again be fortunate enough to load our little fishing-sloop with ivory, instead of cod, herring, mackerel and salmon.

We put in at Hammerfest, latitude seventy-one degrees and forty minutes, for a few days' rest. Here we remained one week, laying in an extra supply of provisions and several casks of drinking-water, and then sailed toward Spitzbergen.

For the first few days we had an open sea and a favoring wind, and then we encountered much ice and many icebergs. A vessel larger than our little fishing-sloop could not possibly have threaded its way among the labyrinth of icebergs or squeezed through the barely open channels. These monster bergs presented an endless succession of crystal palaces, of massive cathedrals and fantastic mountain ranges, grim and sentinel-like, immovable as some towering cliff of solid rock, standing; silent as a sphinx, resisting the restless waves of a fretful sea.

After many narrow escapes, we arrived at Spitzbergen on the 23d of June, and anchored at Wijade Bay for a short time, where we were quite successful in our catches. We then lifted anchor and sailed through the Hinlopen Strait, and coasted along the North-East-Land.[2]

[2 It will be remembered that Andree started on his fatal balloon voyage from the northwest coast of Spitzbergen.]

A strong wind came up from the south-west, and my father said that we had better take advantage of it and try to reach Franz Josef Land, where, the year before he had, by accident, found the ivory tusks that had brought him such a good price at Stock-holm.

Never, before or since, have I seen so many sea-fowl; they were so numerous that they hid the rocks on the coast line and darkened the sky.

For several days we sailed along the rocky coast of Franz Josef Land. Finally, a favoring wind came up that enabled us to make the West Coast, and, after sailing twenty-four hours, we came to a beautiful inlet.

One could hardly believe it was the far Northland. The place was green with grow-ing vegetation, and while the area did not comprise more than one or two acres, yet the air was warm and tranquil. It seemed to be at that point where the Gulf Stream's influence is most keenly felt.[3]

[3 Sir John Barrow, Bart., F.R.S., in his work entitled "Voyages of Discovery and Research Within the Arctic Regions," says on page 57: "Mr. Beechey refers to what has frequently been found and noticed — the mildness of the temperature on the western coast of Spitzbergen, there being little or no sensation of cold, though the thermometer might be only a few degrees above the freezing-point. The brilliant and lively effect of a clear day, when the sun shines forth with a pure sky, whose azure hue is so intense as to find no parallel even in the boasted Italian sky."]

On the east coast there were numerous icebergs, yet here we were in open water. Far to the west of us, however, were icepacks, and still farther to the westward the ice appeared like ranges of low hills. In front of us, and directly to the north, lay an open sea.[4]

[4 Captain Kane, on page 299, quoting from Morton's Journal on Monday, the 26th

of December, says: "As far as I could see, the open passages were fifteen miles or more wide, with sometimes mashed ice separating them. But it is all small ice, and I think it either drives out to the open space to the north or rots and sinks, as I could see none ahead to the north."]

My father was an ardent believer in Odin and Thor, and had frequently told me they were gods who came from far beyond the "North Wind."

There was a tradition, my father explained, that still farther northward was a land more beautiful than any that mortal man had ever known, and that it was inhabited by the "Chosen."[5]

[5 We find the following in "Deutsche Mythologie," page 778, from the pen of Jakob Grimm; "Then, the sons of Bor built in the middle of the universe the city called Asgard, where dwell the gods and their kindred, and from that abode work out so many wondrous things both on the earth and in the heavens above it. There is in that city a place called Illidskjalf, and when Odin is seated there upon his lofty throne he sees over the

whole world and discerns all the actions of men."]

My youthful imagination was fired by the ardor, zeal and religious fervor of my good father, and I exclaimed: "Why not sail to this goodly land? The sky is fair, the wind favorable and the sea open."

Even now I can see the expression of pleasurable surprise on his countenance as he turned toward me and asked: "My son, are you willing to go with me and explore — to go far beyond where man has ever ventured?" I answered affirmatively. "Very well," he replied. "May the god Odin protect us!" and, quickly adjusting the sails, he glanced at our compass, turned the prow in due northerly direction through an open channel, and our voyage had begun.[6]

[6 Hall writes, on page 288: "On the 23rd of January the two Esquimaux, accompanied by two of the seamen, went to Cape Lupton. They reported a sea of open water extending as far as the eye could reach."]

The sun was low in the horizon, as it was still the early summer. Indeed, we had almost four months of day ahead of us before the frozen night could come on again.

Our little fishing-sloop sprang forward as if eager as ourselves for adventure. Within thirty-six hours we were out of sight of the highest point on the coast line of Franz Josef Land. "We seemed to be in a strong current running north by northeast. Far to the right and to the left of us were icebergs, but our little sloop bore down on the narrows and passed through channels and out into open seas — channels so narrow in places that, had our craft been other than small, we never could have gotten through.

On the third day we came to an island. Its shores were washed by an open sea. My father determined to land and explore for a day. This new land was destitute of timber, but we found a large accumulation of drift-wood on the northern shore. Some of the trunks of the trees were forty feet long and two feet in diameter.[7]

[7 Greely tells us in vol. 1, page 100, that: "Privates Connell and Frederick found a large coniferous tree on the beach, just

above the extreme high-water mark. It was nearly thirty inches in circumference, some thirty feet long, and had apparently been carried to that point by a current within a couple of years. A portion of it was cut up for fire-wood, and for the first time in that valley, a bright, cheery camp-fire gave comfort to man."]

After one day's exploration of the coast line of this island, we lifted anchor and turned our prow to the north in an open sea.[8]

[8 Dr. Kane says, on page 379 of his works: "I cannot imagine what becomes of the ice. A strong current sets in constantly to the north; but, from altitudes of more than five hundred feet, I saw only narrow strips of ice, with great spaces of open water, from ten to fifteen miles in breadth, between them. It must, therefore, either go to an open space in the north, or dissolve."]

I remember that neither my father nor myself had tasted food for almost thirty hours. Perhaps this was because of the tension of excitement about our strange voyage in waters farther north, my father said, than anyone had ever before been. Active mentality had dulled the demands of the physical needs.

Instead of the cold being intense as we had anticipated, it was really warmer and more pleasant than it had been while in Hammerfest on the north coast of Norway, some six weeks before.[9]

[9 Captain Peary's second voyage relates another circumstance which may serve to confirm a conjecture which has long been maintained by some, that an open sea, free of ice, exists at or near the Pole. "On the second of November," says Peary, "the wind freshened up to a gale from north by west, lowered the thermometer before midnight to 5 degrees, whereas, a rise of wind at Melville Island was generally accompanied by a simultaneous rise in the thermometer at low temperatures. May not this," he asks, "be occasioned by the wind blowing over an open sea in the quarter from which the wind blows? And tend to confirm the opinion that at or near the Pole an open sea exists?"]

We both frankly admitted that we were

very hungry, and forthwith I prepared a substantial meal from our well-stored larder. When we had partaken heartily of the repast, I told my father I believed I would sleep, as I was beginning to feel quite drowsy. "Very well," he replied, "I will keep the watch."

I have no way to determine how long I slept; I only know that I was rudely awakened by a terrible commotion of the sloop. To my surprise, I found my father sleeping soundly. I cried out lustily to him, and starting up, he sprang quickly to his feet. Indeed, had he not instantly clutched the rail, he would certainly have been thrown into the seething waves.

A fierce snow-storm was raging. The wind was directly astern, driving our sloop at a terrific speed, and was threatening every moment to capsize us. There was no time to lose, the sails had to be lowered immediately. Our boat was writhing in convulsions. A few icebergs we knew were on either side of us, but fortunately the channel was open directly to the north. But would it remain so? In front of us, girding the horizon from left to right, was a vaporish fog or mist, black as Egyptian night at the water's edge, and white like a steam-cloud toward the top, which was finally lost to view as it blended with the great white flakes of falling snow. Whether it covered a treacherous iceberg, or some other hidden obstacle against which our little sloop would dash and send us to a watery grave, or was merely the phenomenon of an Arctic fog, there was no way to determine.[10]

[10 On page 284 of his works, Hall writes: "From the top of Providence Berg, a dark fog was seen to the north, indicating water. At 10 a. m. three of the men (Kruger, Nindemann and Hobby) went to Cape Lupton to ascertain if possible the extent of the open water. On their return they reported several open spaces and much young ice — not more than a day old, so thin that it was easily broken by throwing pieces of ice upon it."]

By what miracle we escaped being dashed to utter destruction, I do not know. I remember our little craft creaked and groaned, as if its joints were breaking. It rocked and staggered to and fro as if clutched by some fierce undertow of whirlpool or maelstrom.

Fortunately our compass had been fastened with long screws to a crossbeam. Most of our provisions, however, were tumbled out and swept away from the deck of the cuddy, and had we not taken the precaution at the very beginning to tie ourselves firmly to the masts of the sloop, we should have been swept into the lashing sea.

Above the deafening tumult of the raging waves, I heard my father's voice. "Be courageous, my son," he shouted, "Odin is the god of the waters, the companion of the brave, and he is with us. Fear not."

To me it seemed there was no possibility of our escaping a horrible death. The little sloop was shipping water, the snow was falling so fast as to be blinding, and the waves were tumbling over our counters in reckless white-sprayed fury. There was no telling what instant we should be dashed against some drifting ice-pack. The tremendous swells would heave us up to the very peaks of mountainous waves, then plunge us down into the depths of the sea's trough as if our fishing-sloop were a fragile shell. Gigantic white-capped waves, like veritable walls, fenced us in, fore and aft.

This terrible nerve-racking ordeal, with its nameless horrors of suspense and agony of fear indescribable, continued for more than three hours, and all the time we were being driven forward at fierce speed. Then suddenly, as if growing weary of its frantic exertions, the wind began to lessen its fury and by degrees to die down.

At last we were in a perfect calm. The fog mist had also disappeared, and before us lay an iceless channel perhaps ten or fifteen miles wide, with a few icebergs far away to our right, and an intermittent archipelago of smaller ones to the left.

I watched my father closely, determined to remain silent until he spoke. Presently he untied the rope from his waist and, without saying a word, began working the pumps, which fortunately were not damaged, relieving the sloop of the water it had shipped in the madness of the storm.

He put up the sloop's sails as calmly as if casting a fishing-net, and then remarked that we were ready for a favoring wind when it came. His courage and persistence were truly remarkable.

On investigation we found less than one-third of our provisions remaining, while to our utter dismay, we discovered that our water-casks had been swept overboard during the violent plungings of our boat.

Two of our water-casks were in the main hold, but both were empty. We had a fair supply of food, but no fresh water. I realized at once the awfulness of our position. Presently I was seized with a consuming thirst. "It is indeed bad," remarked my father. "However, let us dry our bedraggled clothing, for we are soaked to the skin. Trust to the god Odin, my son. Do not give up hope."

The sun was beating down slantingly, as if we were in a southern latitude, instead of in the far Northland. It was swinging around, its orbit ever visible and rising higher and higher each day, frequently mist-covered, yet always peering through the lacework of clouds like some fretful eye of fate, guarding the mysterious Northland and jealously watching the pranks of man. Far to our right the rays decking the prisms of icebergs were gorgeous. Their reflections emitted flashes of garnet, of diamond, of sapphire. A pyrotechnic panorama of countless colors and shapes, while below could be seen the green-tinted sea, and above, the purple sky.

PART THREE

BEYOND THE NORTH WIND

I TRIED to forget my thirst by busying myself with bringing up some food and an empty vessel from the hold. Reaching over the side-rail, I filled the vessel with water for the purpose of laving my hands and face. To my astonishment, when the water came in contact with my lips, I could taste no salt. I was startled by the discovery. "Father!" I fairly gasped, "the water, the water; it is fresh!" "What, Olaf?" exclaimed my father, glancing hastily around. "Surely you are mistaken. There is no land. You are going mad." "But taste it!" I cried.

And thus we made the discovery that the water was indeed fresh, absolutely so, without the least briny taste or even the suspicion of a salty flavor.

We forthwith filled our two remaining water-casks, and my father declared it was a heavenly dispensation of mercy from the gods Odin and Thor.

We were almost beside ourselves with joy, but hunger bade us end our enforced fast. Now that we had found fresh water in the open sea, what might we not expect in this strange latitude where ship had never before sailed and the splash of an oar had never been heard? [11]

[11 In vol. I, page 196, Nansen writes: "It is a peculiar phenomenon,— this dead water. We had at present a better opportunity of studying it than we desired. It occurs where a surface layer of fresh water rests upon the salt water of the sea, and this fresh water is carried along with the ship gliding on the heavier sea beneath it as if on a fixed foundation. The difference between the two strata was in this case so great that while we had drinking water on the surface, the water we got from the bottom cock of the engine-room was far too salt to be used for the boiler."]

We had scarcely appeased our hunger when a breeze began filling the idle sails, and, glancing at the compass, we found the northern point pressing hard against the glass.

In response to my surprise, my father said, "I have heard of this before; it is what they call the dipping of the needle."

We loosened the compass and turned it at right angles with the surface of the sea before its point would free itself from the glass and point according to unmolested attraction. It shifted uneasily, and seemed as unsteady as a drunken man, but finally pointed a course.

Before this we thought the wind was carrying us north by northwest, but, with the needle free, we discovered, if it could be relied upon, that we were sailing slightly north by northeast. Our course, however, was ever tending northward.[12]

[12 In volume II, pages 18 and 19, Nansen writes about the inclination of the needle. Speaking of Johnson, his aide: "One day — it was November 24 — he came in to supper

a little after six o'clock, quite alarmed, and said: 'There has just been a singular inclination of the needle in twenty-four degrees. And remarkably enough, its northern extremity pointed to the east.'"

We again find in Peary's first voyage — page 67,— the following: "It had been observed that from the moment they had entered Lancaster Sound, the motion of the compass needle was very sluggish, and both this and its deviation increased as they progressed to the westward, and continued to do so in descending this inlet. Having reached latitude 73 degrees, they witnessed for the first time the curious phenomenon of the directive power of the needle becoming so weak as to be completely overcome by the attraction of the ship, so that the needle might now be said to point to the north pole of the ship."]

The sea was serenely smooth, with hardly a choppy wave, and the wind brisk and exhilarating. The sun's rays, while striking us aslant, furnished tranquil warmth. And thus time wore on day after day, and we found from the record in our logbook, we had been sailing eleven days since the storm in the open sea.

By strictest economy, our food was holding out fairly well, but beginning to run low. In the meantime, one of our casks of water had been exhausted, and my father said: "We will fill it again." But, to our dismay, we found the water was now as salt as in the region of the Lofoden Islands off the coast of Norway. This necessitated our being extremely careful of the remaining cask.

I found myself wanting to sleep much of the time; whether it was the effect of the exciting experience of sailing in unknown waters, or the relaxation from the awful excitement incident to our adventure in a storm at sea, or due to want of food, I could not say.

I frequently lay down on the bunker of our little sloop, and looked far up into the blue dome of the sky; and, notwithstanding the sun was shining far away in the east, I always saw a single star overhead. For several days, when I looked for this star, it was always there directly above us.

It was now, according to our reckoning, about the first of August. The sun was high in the heavens, and was so bright that I could no longer see the one lone star that attracted my attention a few days earlier.

One day about this time, my father startled me by calling my attention to a novel sight far in front of us, almost at the horizon. "It is a mock sun," exclaimed my father. "I have read of them; it is called a reflection or mirage. It will soon pass away."

But this dull-red,

false sun, as we supposed it to be, did not pass away for several hours; and while we were unconscious of its emitting any rays of light, still there was no time thereafter when we could not sweep the horizon in front and locate the illumination of the so-called false sun, during a period of at least twelve hours out of every twenty-four.

Clouds and mists would at times almost, but never entirely, hide its location. Gradually it seemed to climb higher in the horizon of the uncertain purply sky as we advanced.

It could hardly be said to resemble the sun, except in its circular shape, and when not obscured by clouds or the ocean mists, it had a hazy-red, bronzed appearance, which would change to a white light like a luminous cloud, as if reflecting some greater light beyond.

"We finally agreed in our discussion of this smoky furnace-colored sun, that, whatever the cause of the phenomenon, it was not a reflection of our sun, but a planet of some sort — a reality.[13]

[13 Nansen, on page 394, says: "To-day another noteworthy thing happened, which was that about mid-day we saw the sun, or to be more correct, an image of the sun, for it was only a mirage. A peculiar impression was produced by the sight of that glowing fire lit just above the outermost edge of the ice. According to the enthusiastic descriptions given by many Arctic travelers of the first appearance of this god of life after the long winter night, the impression ought to be one of jubilant excitement; but it was not so in my case. We had not expected to see it for some days yet, so that my feeling was rather one of pain, of disappointment that we must have drifted farther south than we thought. So it was with pleasure I soon discovered that it could not be the sun itself. The mirage was at first a flattened-out, glowing red, streak of fire on the horizon; later there were two streaks, the one above the other, with a dark space between; and from the maintop I could see four, or even five, such horizontal lines directly over one another, all of equal length, as if one could only imagine a square, dull-red sun, with horizontal dark streaks across it."]

One day soon after this, I felt exceedingly drowsy, and fell into a sound sleep. But it seemed that I was almost immediately aroused by my father's vigorous shaking of me by the shoulder and saying: "Olaf, awaken; there is land in sight!"

I sprang to my feet, and oh! joy unspeakable! There, far in the distance, yet directly in our path, were lands jutting boldly into the sea. The shore-line stretched far away to the right of us, as far as the eye could see, and all along the sandy beach were waves breaking into choppy foam, receding, then going forward again, ever chanting in monotonous thunder tones the song of the deep. The banks were covered with trees and vegetation.

I cannot express my feeling of exultation at this discovery. My father stood motionless, with his hand on the tiller, looking straight ahead, pouring out his heart in thankful prayer and thanksgiving to the gods Odin and Thor.

In the meantime, a net which we found in the stowage had been cast, and we caught a few fish that materially added to our dwindling stock of provisions.

The compass, which we had fastened back in its place, in fear of another storm, was still pointing due north, and moving on its pivot, just as it had at Stockholm. The dipping of the needle had ceased. What could this mean? Then, too, our many days of sailing had certainly carried us far past the North Pole. And yet the needle continued to point north. We were sorely perplexed, for surely our direction was now south.[14]

[14 Peary's first voyage, pages 69 and 70, says: "On reaching Sir Byam Martin's Island, the nearest to Melville Island, the latitude of the place of observation was 75 degrees - 09' - 23", and the longitude 103 degrees - 44' - 37"; the dip of the magnetic needle 88 degrees - 25' - 56" west in the longitude of 91 degrees - 48', where the last observations on the shore had been made, to 165 degrees - 50' - 09", east, at their present station, so thatwe had," says Peary, "in sailing over the space included between these two meridians, crossed immediately northward of the magnetic pole, and had undoubtedly passed

over one of those spots upon the globe where the needle would have been found to vary 180 degrees, or in other words, where the North Pole would have pointed to the south."]

We sailed for three days along the shoreline, then came to the mouth of a fjord or river of immense size. It seemed more like a great bay, and into this we turned our fishing-craft, the direction being slightly northeast of south. By the assistance of a fretful wind that came to our aid about twelve hours out of every twenty-four, we continued to make our way inland, into what afterward proved to be a mighty river, and which we learned was called by the inhabitants Hiddekel.

We continued our journey for ten days thereafter, and found we had fortunately attained a distance inland where ocean tides no longer affected the water, which had become fresh.

The discovery came none too soon, for our remaining cask of water was well-nigh exhausted. We lost no time in replenishing our casks, and continued to sail farther up the river when the wind was favorable.

Along the banks great forests miles in extent could be seen stretching away on the shore-line. The trees were of enormous size. We landed after anchoring near a sandy beach, and waded ashore, and were rewarded by finding a quantity of nuts that were very palatable and satisfying to hunger, and a welcome change from the monotony of our stock of provisions.

It was about the first of September, over five months, we calculated, since our leave-taking from Stockholm. Suddenly we were frightened almost out of our wits by hearing in the far distance the singing of people. Very soon thereafter we discovered a huge ship gliding down the river directly toward us. Those aboard were singing in one mighty chorus that, echoing from bank to bank, sounded like a thousand voices, filling the whole universe with quivering melody. The accompaniment was played on stringed instruments not unlike our harps.

It was a larger ship than any we had ever seen, and was differently constructed.[15]

[15 Asiatic Mythology,—page 240, "Para-

dise found" — from translation by Sayce, in a book called "Records of the Past," we were told of a "dwelling" which "the gods created for" the first human beings,— a dwelling in which they "became great" and "increased in numbers," and the location of which is described in words exactly corresponding to those of Iranian, Indian, Chinese, Eddaic and Aztecan literature; namely, "in the center of the earth." — Warren.]

At this particular time our sloop was becalmed, and not far from the shore. The bank of the river, covered with mammoth trees, rose up several hundred feet in beautiful fashion. We seemed to be on the edge of some primeval forest that doubtless stretched far inland.

The immense craft paused, and almost immediately a boat was lowered and six men of gigantic stature rowed to our little fishing-sloop. They spoke to us in a strange language. We knew from their manner, however, that they were not unfriendly. They talked a great deal among themselves, and one of them laughed immoderately, as though in finding us a queer discovery had been made. One of them spied our compass, and it seemed to interest them more than any other part of our sloop.

Finally, the leader motioned as if to ask whether we were willing to leave our craft to go on board their ship. "What say you, my son?" asked my father. "They cannot do any more than kill us."

"They seem to be kindly disposed," I replied, "although what terrible giants! They must be the select six of the kingdom's crack regiment. Just look at their great size."

"We may as well go willingly as be taken by force," said my father, smiling, "for they are certainly able to capture us." Thereupon he made known, by signs, that we were ready to accompany them.

Within a few minutes we were on board the ship, and half an hour later our little fishing-craft had been lifted bodily out of the water by a strange sort of hook and tackle, and set on board as a curiosity.

There were several hundred people on board this, to us, mammoth ship, which we discovered was called "The Naz," meaning, as we afterward learned, "Pleasure," or to give a more proper interpretation, "Pleasure Excursion" ship.

If my father and I were curiously observed by the ship's occupants, this strange race of giants offered us an equal amount of wonderment.

There was not a single man aboard who would not have measured fully twelve feet in height. They all wore full beards, not particularly long, but seemingly short-cropped. They had mild and beautiful faces, exceedingly fair, with ruddy complexions. The hair and beard of some were black, others sandy, and still others yellow. The captain, as we designated the dignitary in command of the great vessel, was fully a head taller than any of his companions. The women averaged from ten to eleven feet in height. Their features were especially regular and refined, while their complexion was of a most delicate tint heightened by a healthful glow.[16]

[16 "According to all procurable data, that spot at the era of man's appearance upon the stage was in the now lost 'Miocene continent,' which then surrounded the Arctic Pole. That in that true, original Eden some of the early generations of men attained to a stature and longevity unequaled in any countries known to postdiluvian history is by no means scientifically incredible." — Wm. F. Warren, "Paradise Found," p. 284.]

Both men and women seemed to possess that particular ease of manner which we deem a sign of good breeding, and, notwithstanding their huge statures, there was nothing about them suggesting awkwardness. As I was a lad in only my nineteenth year, I was doubtless looked upon as a true Tom Thumb. My father's six feet three did not lift the top of his head above the waist line of these people.

Each one seemed to vie with the others in extending courtesies and showing kindness to us, but all laughed heartily, I remember, when they had to improvise chairs for my father and myself to sit at table. They were richly attired in a costume peculiar to themselves, and very attractive. The men were clothed in handsomely embroidered tunics of silk and satin and belted at the waist. They wore knee-breeches and stockings of a fine texture, while their feet were encased in sandals adorned with gold buckles. We early discovered that gold was one of the most common metals known, and that it was used extensively in decoration.

Strange as it may seem, neither my father nor myself felt the least bit of solicitude for our safety. "We have come into our own," my father said to me. "This is the fulfillment of the tradition told me by my father and my father's father, and still back for many generations of our race. This is, assuredly, the land beyond the North Wind."

We seemed to make such an impression on the party that we were given specially into the charge of one of the men, Jules Galdea, and his wife, for the purpose of being educated in their language; and we, on our part, were just as eager to learn as they were to instruct.

At the captain's command, the vessel was swung cleverly about, and began retracing its course up the river. The machinery, while noiseless, was very powerful.

The banks and trees on either side seemed to rush by. The ship's speed, at times, surpassed that of any railroad train on which I have ever ridden, even here in America. It was wonderful.

In the meantime we had lost sight of the sun's rays, but we found a radiance "within" emanating from the dull-red sun which had already attracted our attention, now giving out a white light seemingly from a cloud-bank far away in front of us. It dispensed a greater light, I should say, than two full moons on the clearest night.

In twelve hours this cloud of whiteness would pass out of sight as if eclipsed, and the twelve hours following corresponded with our night. We early learned that these strange people were worshipers of this great cloud of night. It was "The Smoky God" of the "Inner World."

The ship was equipped with a mode of illumination which I now presume was electricity, but neither my father nor myself were sufficiently skilled in mechanics to understand whence came the power to operate the ship, or to maintain the soft beautiful lights that answered the same purpose of our present methods of lighting the streets of our cities, our houses and places of business.

It must be remembered, the time of

which I write was the autumn of 1829, and we of the "outside" surface of the earth knew nothing then, so to speak, of electricity.

The electrically surcharged condition of the air was a constant vitalizer. I never felt better in my life than during the two years my father and I sojourned on the inside of the earth.

To resume my narrative of events; The ship on which we were sailing came to a stop two days after we had been taken on board. My father said as nearly as he could judge, we were directly under Stockholm or London. The city we had reached was called "Jehu," signifying a seaport town. The houses were large and beautifully constructed, and quite uniform in appearance, yet without sameness. The principal occupation of the people appeared to be agriculture; the hillsides were covered with vineyards, while the valleys were devoted to the growing of grain.

I never saw such a display of gold. It was everywhere. The door-casings were inlaid and the tables were veneered with sheetings of gold. Domes of the public buildings were of gold. It was used most generously in the finishings of the great temples of music.

Vegetation grew in lavish exuberance, and fruit of all kinds possessed the most delicate flavor. Clusters of grapes four and five feet in length, each grape as large as an orange, and apples larger than a man's head typified the wonderful growth of all things on the "inside" of the earth.

The great redwood trees of California would be considered mere underbrush compared with the giant forest trees extending for miles and miles in all directions. In many directions along the foothills of the mountains vast herds of cattle were seen during the last day of our travel on the river.

"We heard much of a city called "Eden," but were kept at "Jehu" for an entire year. By the end of that time we had learned to speak fairly well the language of this strange race of people. Our instructors, Jules Galdea and his wife, exhibited a patience that was truly commendable.

One day an envoy from the Ruler at "Eden" came to see us, and for two whole days my father and myself were put through a series of surprising questions. They wished to know from whence we came, what sort of people dwelt "without," what God we worshiped, our religious beliefs, the mode of living in our strange land, and a thousand other things.

The compass which we had brought with us attracted especial attention. My father and I commented between ourselves on the fact that the compass still pointed north, although we now knew that we had sailed over the curve or edge of the earth's aperture, and were far along southward on the "inside" surface of the earth's crust, which, according to my father's estimate and my own, is about three hundred miles in thickness from the "inside" to the "outside" surface. Relatively speaking, it is no thicker than an egg-shell, so that there is almost as much surface on the "inside" as on the "outside" of the earth.

The great luminous cloud or ball of dull-red fire — fiery-red in the mornings and evenings, and during the day giving off a beautiful white light, "The Smoky God," — is seemingly suspended in the center of the great vacuum "within" the earth, and held to its place by the immutable law of gravitation, or a repellant atmospheric force, as the case may be. I refer to the known power that draws or repels with equal force in all directions.

The base of this electrical cloud or central luminary, the seat of the gods, is dark and non-transparent, save for innumerable small openings, seemingly in the bottom of the great support or altar of the Deity, upon which "The Smoky God" rests; and, the lights shining through these many openings twinkle at night in all their splendor, and seem to be stars, as natural as the stars we saw shining when in our home at Stockholm, excepting that they appear larger. "The Smoky God," therefore, with each daily revolution of the earth, appears to come up in the east and go down in the west, the same as does our sun on the external surface. In reality, the people "within" believe that "The Smoky God" is the throne of their Jehovah, and is stationary. The effect of night and day is, therefore, produced by the earth's daily rotation.

I have since discovered that the language of the people of the Inner World is much like the Sanskrit.

After we had given an account of ourselves to the emissaries from the central seat of government of the inner continent, and my father had, in his crude way, drawn maps, at their request, of the "outside" surface of the earth, showing the divisions of land and water, and giving the name of each of the continents, large islands and the oceans, we were taken overland to the city of "Eden," in a conveyance different from anything we have in Europe or America. This vehicle was doubtless some electrical contrivance. It was noiseless, and ran on a single iron rail in perfect balance. The trip was made at a very high rate of speed. We were carried up hills and down dales, across valleys and again along the sides of steep mountains, without any apparent attempt having been made to level the earth as we do for railroad tracks. The car seats were huge yet comfortable affairs, and very high above the floor of the car. On the top of each car were high geared fly wheels lying on their sides, which were so automatically adjusted that, as the speed of the car increased, the high speed of these fly wheels geometrically increased. Jules Galdea explained to us that these revolving fan-like wheels on top of the cars destroyed atmospheric pressure, or what is generally understood by the term gravitation, and with this force thus destroyed or rendered nugatory the car is as safe from falling to one side or the other from the single rail track as if it were in a vacuum; the fly wheels in their rapid revolutions destroying effectually the so-called power of gravitation, or the force of atmospheric pressure or whatever potent influence it may be that causes all unsupported things to fall downward to the earth's surface or to the nearest point of resistance.

The surprise of my father and myself was indescribable when, amid the regal magnificence of a spacious hall, we were finally brought before the Great High Priest, ruler over all the land. He was richly robed, and much taller than those about him, and could not have been less than fourteen or fifteen feet in height. The immense room in which we were received seemed finished in solid slabs of gold thickly studded with jewels, of amazing brilliancy.

The city of "Eden" is located in what seems to be a beautiful valley, yet, in fact, it is on the loftiest mountain plateau of the Inner Continent, several thousand feet higher than any portion of the surrounding country. It is the most beautiful place I have ever beheld in all my travels. In this elevated garden all manner of fruits, vines, shrubs, trees, and flowers grow in riotous profusion.

In this garden four rivers have their source in a mighty artesian fountain. They divide and flow in four directions. This place is called by the inhabitants the "navel of the earth," or the beginning, "the cradle of the human race." The names of the rivers are the Euphrates, the Pison, the Gihon, and the Hiddekel.[17]

[17 "And the Lord God planted a garden, and out of the ground made the Lord God to grow every tree that is pleasant to the sight

and good for food." — The Book of Genesis.]

The unexpected awaited us in this palace of beauty, in the finding of our little fishing-craft. It had been brought before the High Priest in perfect shape, just as it had been taken from the waters that day when it was loaded on board the ship by the people who discovered us on the river more than a year before.

"We were given an audience of over two hours with this great dignitary, who seemed kindly disposed and considerate. He showed himself eagerly interested, asking us numerous questions, and invariably regarding things about which his emissaries had failed to inquire.

At the conclusion of the interview he inquired our pleasure, asking us whether we wished to remain in his country or if we preferred to return to the "outer" world, providing it were possible to make a successful return trip, across the frozen belt barriers that encircle both the northern and southern openings of the earth.

My father replied: "It would please me and my son to visit your country and see your people, your colleges and palaces of music and art, your great fields, your wonderful forests of timber; and after we have had this pleasurable privilege, we should like to try to return to our home on the 'outside' surface of the earth. This son is my only child, and my good wife will be weary awaiting our return."

"I fear you can never return," replied the

Chief High Priest, "because the way is a most hazardous one. However, you shall visit the different countries with Jules Galdea as your escort, and be accorded every courtesy and kindness. Whenever you are ready to attempt a return voyage, I assure you that your boat which is here on exhibition shall be put in the waters of the river Hiddekel at its mouth, and we will bid you Jehovah-speed."

Thus terminated our only interview with the High Priest or Ruler of the continent.

PART FOUR

IN THE UNDER WORLD

WE learned that the males do not marry before they are from seventy-five to one hundred years old, and that the age at which women enter wedlock is only a little less, and that both men and women frequently live to be from six to eight hundred years old, and in some instances much older.[18]

[18 Josephus says: "God prolonged the life of the patriarchs that preceded the deluge, both on account of their virtues and to give them the opportunity of perfecting the sciences of geometry and astronomy, which they had discovered; which they could not have done if they had not lived 600 years, because it is only after the lapse of 600 years

that the great year is accomplished." — Flammarion, Astronomical Myths, Paris p. 26.]

During the following year we visited many villages and towns, prominent among them being the cities of Nigi, Delfi, Hectea, and my father was called upon no less than a half-dozen times to go over the maps which had been made from the rough sketches he had originally given of the divisions of land and water on the "outside" surface of the earth.

I remember hearing my father remark that the giant race of people in the land of "The Smoky God" had almost as accurate an idea of the geography of the "outside" surface of the earth as had the average college professor in Stockholm.

In our travels we came to a forest of gigantic trees, near the city of Delfi. Had the Bible said there were trees towering over three hundred feet in height, and more than thirty feet in diameter, growing in the Garden of Eden, the Ingersolls, the Tom Paines and Voltaires would doubtless have pronounced the statement a myth. Yet this is the description of the California sequoia gigantea; but these California giants pale into insignificance when compared with the forest Goliaths found in the "within" continent, where abound mighty trees from eight hundred to one thousand feet in height, and from one hundred to one hundred and twenty feet in diameter; countless in numbers and forming forests extending hundreds of miles back from the sea.

The people are exceedingly musical, and learned to a remarkable degree in their arts and sciences, especially geometry and astronomy. Their cities are equipped with vast palaces of music, where not infrequently as many as twenty-five thousand lusty voices of this giant race swell forth in mighty choruses of the most sublime symphonies.

The children are not supposed to attend institutions of learning before they are twenty years old. Then their school life begins and continues for thirty years, ten of which are uniformly devoted by both sexes to the study of music.

Their principal vocations are architecture, agriculture, horticulture, the raising of vast herds of cattle, and the building of conveyances peculiar to that country, for travel on land and water. By some device which I cannot explain, they hold communion with one another between the most distant parts of their country, on air currents.

All buildings are erected with special regard to strength, durability, beauty and symmetry, and with a style of architecture vastly more attractive to the eye than any I have ever observed elsewhere.

About three-fourths of the "inner" surface of the earth is land and about one-fourth water. There are numerous rivers of tremendous size, some flowing in a northerly direction and others southerly. Some of these rivers are thirty miles in width, and it is out of these vast waterways, at the extreme northern and southern parts of the "inside" surface of the earth, in regions where low temperatures are experienced, that fresh-water icebergs are formed. They are then pushed out to sea like huge tongues of ice, by the abnormal freshets of turbulent waters that, twice every year, sweep everything before them.

We saw innumerable specimens of bird-life no larger than those encountered in the forests of Europe or America. It is well known that during the last few years whole species of birds have quit the earth. A writer in a recent article on this subject says:[19]

[19 "Almost every year sees the final extinction of one or more bird species. Out of fourteen varieties of birds found a century since on a single island — the West Indian island of St. Thomas — eight have now to be numbered among the missing."]

Is it not possible that these disappearing bird species quit their habitation without, and find an asylum in the "within world"?

Whether inland among the mountains, or along the seashore, we found bird life prolific. When they spread their great wings some of the birds appeared to measure thirty feet from tip to tip. They are of great variety and many colors. We were permitted to climb up on the edge of a rock and examine a nest of eggs. There were five in the nest, each of which was at least two feet in length and fifteen inches in diameter.

After we had been in the city of Hectea about a week, Professor Galdea took us to an inlet, where we saw thousands of tortoises along the sandy shore. I hesitate to state the size of these great creatures. They were from twenty-five to thirty feet in length, from fifteen to twenty feet in width and fully seven feet in height. When one of them projected its head it had the appearance of some hideous sea monster.

The strange conditions "within" are favorable not only for vast meadows of luxuriant grasses, forests of giant trees, and all manner of vegetable life, but wonderful animal life as well.

One day we saw a great herd of elephants. There must have been five hundred of these thunder-throated monsters, with their restlessly waving trunks. They were tearing huge boughs from the trees and trampling smaller growth into dust like so much hazel-brush. They would average over 100 feet in length and from 75 to 85 in height.

It seemed, as I gazed upon this wonderful herd of giant elephants, that I was again living in the public library at Stockholm, where I had spent much time studying the wonders of the Miocene age. I was filled with mute astonishment, and my father was speechless with awe. He held my arm with a protecting grip, as if fearful harm would overtake us. We were two atoms in this great forest, and, fortunately, unobserved by this vast herd of elephants as they drifted on and away, following a leader as does a herd of sheep. They browsed from growing herbage which they encountered as they traveled, and now and again shook the firmament with their deep bellowing.[20]

[20 "Moreover, there were a great number of elephants in the island: and there was provision for animals of every kind. Also whatever fragrant things there are in the earth, whether roots or herbage, or woods, or distilling drops of flowers or fruits, grew and thrived in that land." — The Cratylus of Plato.]

There is a hazy mist that goes up from

the land each evening, and it invariably rains once every twenty-four hours. This great moisture and the invigorating electrical light and warmth account perhaps for the luxuriant vegetation, while the highly charged electrical air and the evenness of climatic conditions may have much to do with the giant growth and longevity of all animal life.

In places the level valleys stretched away for many miles in every direction. "The Smoky God," in its clear white light, looked calmly down. There was an intoxication in the electrically surcharged air that fanned the cheek as softly as a vanishing whisper. Nature chanted a lullaby in the faint murmur of winds whose breath was sweet with the fragrance of bud and blossom.

After having spent considerably more than a year in visiting several of the many cities of the "within" world and a great deal of intervening country, and more than two years had passed from the time we had been picked up by the great excursion ship on the river, we decided to cast our fortunes once more upon the sea, and endeavor to regain the "outside" surface of the earth.

We made known our wishes, and they were reluctantly but promptly followed. Our hosts gave my father, at his request, various maps showing the entire "inside" surface of the earth, its cities, oceans, seas, rivers, gulfs and bays. They also generously offered to give us all the bags of gold nuggets — some of them as large as a goose's egg — that we were willing to attempt to take with us in our little fishing-boat.

In due time we returned to Jehu, at which place we spent one month in fixing up and overhauling our little fishing sloop. After all was in readiness, the same ship "Naz" that originally discovered us, took us on board and sailed to the mouth of the river Hiddekel.

After our giant brothers had launched our little craft for us, they were most cordially regretful at parting, and evinced much solicitude for our safety. My father swore by the Gods Odin and Thor that he would surely return again within a year or two and pay them another visit. And thus we bade them adieu. We made ready and hoisted our sail, but there was little breeze. We were becalmed within an hour after our giant friends had left us and started on their return trip.

The winds were constantly blowing south, that is, they were blowing from the northern opening of the earth toward that which we knew to be south, but which, according to our compass's pointing finger, was directly north.

For three days we tried to sail, and to beat against the wind, but to no avail. Whereupon my father said: "My son, to return by the same route as we came in is impossible at this time of year. I wonder why we did not think of this before. We have been here almost two and a half years; therefore, this is the season when the sun is beginning to shine in at the southern opening of the earth. The long cold night is on in the Spitzbergen country."

"What shall we do?" I inquired.

"There is only one thing we can do," my

father replied, "and that is to go south." Accordingly, he turned the craft about, gave it full reef, and started by the compass north but, in fact, directly south. The wind was strong, and we seemed to have struck a current that was running with remarkable swiftness in the same direction.

In just forty days we arrived at Delfi, a city we had visited in company with our guides Jules Galdea and his wife, near the mouth of the Gihon river. Here we stopped for two days, and were most hospitably entertained by the same people who had welcomed us on our former visit. We laid in some additional provisions and again set sail, following the needle due north.

On our outward trip we came through a narrow channel which appeared to be a separating body of water between two considerable bodies of land. There was a beautiful beach to our right, and we decided to reconnoiter. Casting anchor, we waded ashore to rest up for a day before continuing the outward hazardous undertaking. We built a fire and threw on some sticks of dry driftwood. While my father was walking along the shore, I prepared a tempting repast from supplies we had provided.

There was a mild, luminous light which my father said resulted from the sun shining in from the south aperture of the earth. That night we slept soundly, and awakened the next morning as refreshed as if we had been in our own beds at Stockholm.

After breakfast we started out on an inland tour of discovery, but had not gone far when we sighted some birds which we recognized at once as belonging to the penguin family.

They are flightless birds, but excellent swimmers and tremendous in size, with white breast, short wings, black head, and long peaked bills. They stand fully nine feet high. They looked at us with little surprise, and presently waddled, rather than walked, toward the water, and swam away in a northerly direction.[21]

[21 "The nights are never so dark at the Poles as in other regions, for the moon and stars seem to possess twice as much light and effulgence. In addition, there is a continu-

ous light, the varied shades and play of which are amongst the strangest phenomena of nature." — Rambrosson's Astronomy.]

The events that occurred during the following hundred or more days beggar description. We were on an open and iceless sea. The month we reckoned to be November or December, and we knew the so-called South Pole was turned toward the sun. Therefore, when passing out and away from the internal electrical light of "The Smoky God" and its genial warmth, we would be met by the light and warmth of the sun, shining in through the south opening of the earth. We were not mistaken.[22]

[22 "The fact that gives the phenomenon of the polar aurora its greatest importance is that the earth becomes self-luminous; that, besides the light which as a planet is received from the central body, it shows a capability of sustaining a luminous process proper to itself." — Humboldt.]

There were times when our little craft, driven by wind that was continuous and persistent, shot through the waters like an arrow. Indeed, had we encountered a hidden rock or obstacle, our little vessel would have been crushed into kindling-wood.

At last we were conscious that the atmosphere was growing decidedly colder, and, a few days later, icebergs were sighted far to the left. My father argued, and correctly, that the winds which filled our sails came from the warm climate "within." The time of the year was certainly most auspicious for us to make our dash for the "outside" world and attempt to scud our fishing sloop through open channels of the frozen zone which surrounds the polar regions.

We were soon amid the ice-packs, and how our little craft got through. the narrow channels and escaped being crushed I know not. The compass behaved in the same drunken and unreliable fashion in passing over the southern curve or edge of the earth's shell as it had done on our inbound trip at the northern entrance. It gyrated, dipped and seemed like a thing possessed.[23]

[23 Captain Sabine, on page 105 in "Voyages in the Arctic Regions," says: "The geo-

graphical determination of the direction and intensity of the magnetic forces at different points of the earth's surface has been regarded as an object worthy of especial research. To examine in different parts of the globe, the declination, inclination and intensity of the magnetic force, and their periodical and secular variations, and mutual relations and dependencies could be duly investigated only in fixed magnetical observatories."]

One day as I was lazily looking over the sloop's side into the clear waters, my father shouted: "Breakers ahead!" Looking up, I saw through a lifting mist a white object that towered several hundred feet high, completely shutting off our advance. We lowered sail immediately, and none too soon. In a moment we found ourselves wedged between two monstrous icebergs. Each was crowding and grinding against its fellow mountain of ice. They were like two gods of war contending for supremacy. We were greatly alarmed. Indeed, we were between the lines of a battle royal; the sonorous thunder of the grinding ice was like the continued volleys of artillery. Blocks of ice larger than a house were frequently lifted up a hundred feet by the mighty force of lateral pressure; they would shudder and rock to and fro for a few seconds, then come crashing down with a deafening roar, and disappear in the foaming waters. Thus, for more than two hours, the contest of the icy giants continued.

It seemed as if the end had come. The ice pressure was terrific, and while we were not caught in the dangerous part of the jam, and were safe for the time being, yet the heaving and rending of tons of ice as it fell splashing here and there into the watery depths filled us with shaking fear.

Finally, to our great joy, the grinding of the ice ceased, and within a few hours the great mass slowly divided, and, as if an act of Providence had been performed, right before us lay an open channel. Should we venture with our little craft into this opening? If the pressure came on again, our little sloop as well as ourselves would be crushed into nothingness. We decided to take the chance, and, accordingly, hoisted our sail to a favoring breeze, and soon started out like a race-horse, running the gauntlet of this unknown narrow channel of open water.

PART FIVE

AMONG THE ICE PACKS

FOR the next forty-five days our time was employed in dodging icebergs and hunting channels; indeed, had we not been favored with a strong south wind and a small boat, I doubt if this story could have ever been given to the world.

At last, there came a morning when my father said: "My son, I think we are to see home. We are almost through the ice. See! the open water lies before us."

However, there were a few icebergs that had floated far northward into the open water still ahead of us on either side, stretching away for many miles. Directly in front of us, and by the compass, which had now righted itself, due north, there was an open sea.

"What a wonderful story we have to tell to the people of Stockholm," continued my father, while a look of pardonable elation lighted up his honest face. "And think of the gold nuggets stowed away in the hold!"

I spoke kind words of praise to my father, not alone for his fortitude and endurance, but also for his courageous daring as a discoverer, and for having made the voyage that now promised a successful end. I was grateful, too, that he had gathered the wealth of gold we were carrying home.

While congratulating ourselves on the goodly supply of provisions and water we still had on hand, and on the dangers we had escaped, we were startled by hearing a most terrific explosion, caused by the tearing apart of a huge mountain of ice. It was a deafening roar like the firing of a thousand cannon. We were sailing at the time with great speed, and happened to be near a monstrous iceberg which to all appearances was as immovable as a rockbound island. It seemed, however, that the iceberg had split and was breaking apart, whereupon the balance of the monster along which we were sailing was destroyed, and it began dipping from us. My father quickly anticipated the danger before I realized its awful possibilities. The iceberg extended down into the water many hundreds of feet, and, as it tipped over, the portion coming up out of the water caught our fishing-craft like a lever on a fulcrum, and threw it into the air as if it had been a foot-ball.

Our boat fell back on the iceberg, that by this time had changed the side next to us for the top. My father was still in the boat, having become entangled in the rigging, while I was thrown some twenty feet away.

I quickly scrambled to my feet and shouted to my father, who answered: "All is well." Just then a realization dawned upon me. Horror upon horror! The blood froze in my veins. The iceberg was still in motion, and its great weight and force in toppling over would cause it to submerge temporarily. I fully realized what a sucking maelstrom it would produce amid the worlds of water on every side. They would rush into the depression in all their fury, like white-fanged wolves eager for human prey.

In this supreme moment of mental anguish, I remember glancing at our boat, which was lying on its side, and wondering if it could possibly right itself, and if my father could escape. Was this the end of our struggles and adventures? Was this death? All these questions flashed through my mind in the fraction of a second, and a moment later I was engaged in a life and death struggle. The ponderous monolith of ice sank below the surface, and the frigid waters gurgled around me in frenzied anger. I was in a saucer, with the waters pouring in on every side. A moment more and I lost consciousness.

When I partially recovered my senses, and roused from the swoon of a half-drowned man, I found myself wet, stiff, and almost frozen, lying on the iceberg. But there was no sign of my father or of our little fishing sloop. The monster berg had recovered itself, and, with its new balance, lifted its head perhaps fifty feet above the waves.

The top of this island of ice was a plateau perhaps half an acre in extent.

I loved my father well, and was grief-stricken at the awfulness of his death. I railed at fate, that I, too, had not been permitted to sleep with him in the depths of the ocean. Finally, I climbed to my feet and looked about me. The purple-domed sky above, the shoreless green ocean beneath, and only an occasional iceberg discernible! My heart sank in hopeless despair. I cautiously picked my way across the berg toward the other side, hoping that our fishing craft had righted itself.

Dared I think it possible that my father still lived? It was but a ray of hope that flamed up in my heart. But the anticipation warmed my blood in my veins and started it rushing like some rare stimulant through every fiber of my body.

I crept close to the precipitous side of the iceberg, and peered far down, hoping, still hoping. Then I made a circle of the berg, scanning every foot of the way, and thus I kept going around and around. One part of my brain was certainly becoming maniacal, while the other part, I believe, and do to this day, was perfectly rational.

I was conscious of having made the circuit a dozen times, and while one part of my intelligence knew, in all reason, there was not a vestige of hope, yet some strange fascinating aberration bewitched and compelled me still to beguile myself with expectation. The other part of my brain seemed to tell me that while there was no possibility of my father being alive, yet, if I quit making the circuitous pilgrimage, if I paused for a single moment, it would be acknowledgment of defeat, and, should I do this, I felt that I should go mad. Thus, hour after hour I walked around and around, afraid to stop and rest, yet physically powerless to continue much longer. Oh! horror of horrors! to be cast away in this wide expanse of waters without food or drink, and only a treacherous iceberg for an abiding place. My heart sank within me, and all semblance of hope was fading into black despair.

Then the hand of the Deliverer was extended, and the death-like stillness of a solitude rapidly becoming unbearable was suddenly broken by the firing of a signal-gun. I looked up in startled amazement, when, I saw, less than a half-mile away, a whaling-vessel bearing down toward me with her sail full set.

Evidently my continued activity on the iceberg had attracted their attention. On drawing near, they put out a boat, and, descending cautiously to the water's edge, I was rescued, and a little later lifted on board the whaling-ship.

I found it was a Scotch whaler, "The Arlington." She had cleared from Dundee in September, and started immediately for the Antarctic, in search of whales. The captain, Angus MacPherson, seemed kindly disposed, but in matters of discipline, as I soon learned, possessed of an iron will. When I attempted to tell him that I had come from the "inside" of the earth, the captain and mate looked at each other, shook their heads, and insisted on my being put in a bunk under strict surveillance of the ship's physician.

I was very weak for want of food, and had not slept for many hours. However, after a few days' rest, I got up one morning and dressed myself without asking permission of the physician or anyone else, and told them that I was as sane as anyone.

The captain sent for me and again questioned me concerning where I had come from, and how I came to be alone on an iceberg in the far off Antarctic Ocean. I replied that I had just come from the "inside" of the earth, and proceeded to tell him how my father and myself had gone in by way of Spitzbergen, and come out by way of the South Pole country, whereupon I was put in irons. I afterward heard the captain tell the mate that I was as crazy as a March hare, and that I must remain in confinement until I was rational enough to give a truthful account of myself.

Finally, after much pleading and many promises, I was released from irons. I then and there decided to invent some story that would satisfy the captain, and never again refer to my trip to the land of "The Smoky God," at least until I was safe among friends.

Within a fortnight I was permitted to go about and take my place as one of the seamen. A little later the captain asked me for an explanation. I told him that my experience had been so horrible that I was fearful of my memory, and begged him to permit me to leave the question unanswered until some time in the future. "I think you are recovering considerably," he said, "but you are not sane yet by a good deal."

"Permit me to do such work as you may assign," I replied, "and if it does not compensate you sufficiently, I will pay you immediately after I reach Stockholm — to the last penny." Thus the matter rested.

On finally reaching Stockholm, as I have already related, I found that my good mother had gone to her reward more than a year before. I have also told how, later, the treachery of a relative landed me in a madhouse, where I remained for twenty-eight years — seemingly unending years — and, still later, after my release, how I returned to the life of a fisherman, following it sedulously for twenty-seven years, then how I came to America, and finally to Los Angeles, California. But all this can be of little interest to the reader. Indeed, it seems to me the climax of my wonderful travels and strange adventures was reached when the Scotch sailing-vessel took me from an iceberg on the Antarctic Ocean.

PART SIX

CONCLUSION

IN concluding this history of my adventures, I wish to state that I firmly believe science is yet in its infancy concerning the cosmology of the earth. There is so much that is unaccounted for by the world's accepted knowledge of to-day, and will ever remain so until the land of "The Smoky God" is known and recognized by our geographers.

It is the land from whence came the great logs of cedar that have been found by explorers in open waters far over the northern edge of the earth's crust, and also the bodies of mammoths whose bones are found in vast beds on the Siberian coast.

Northern explorers have done much. Sir

John Franklin, De Haven Grinnell, Sir John Murray, Kane, Melville, Hall, Nansen, Schwatka, Greely, Peary, Ross, Gerlache, Bernacchi, Andree, Amsden, Amundson and others have all been striving to storm the frozen citadel of mystery.

I firmly believe that Andree and his two brave companions, Strindberg and Fraenckell, who sailed away in the balloon "Oreon" from the northwest coast of Spitzbergen on that Sunday afternoon of July 11, 1897, are now in the "within" world, and doubtless are being entertained, as my father and myself were entertained by the kind-hearted giant race inhabiting the inner Atlantic Continent.

Having, in my humble way, devoted years to these problems, I am well acquainted with the accepted definitions of gravity, as well as the cause of the magnetic needle's attraction, and I am prepared to say that it is my firm belief that the magnetic needle is influenced solely by electric currents which completely envelop the earth like a garment, and that these electric currents in an endless circuit pass out of the southern end of the earth's cylindrical opening, diffusing and spreading themselves over all the "outside" surface, and rushing madly on in their course toward the North Pole. And while these currents seemingly dash off into space at the earth's curve or edge, yet they drop again to the "inside" surface and continue their way southward along the inside of the earth's crust, toward the opening of the so-called South Pole.[24]

[24 "Mr. Lemstrom concluded that an electric discharge which could only be seen by means of the spectroscope was taking place on the surface of the ground all around him, and that from a distance it would appear as a faint display of Aurora, the phenomena of pale and flaming light which is some times seen on the top of the Spitzbergen Mountains." — The Arctic Manual, page 739.]

As to gravity, no one knows what it is, because it has not been determined whether it is atmospheric pressure that causes the apple to fall, or whether, 150 miles below the surface of the earth, supposedly one-half way through the earth's crust, there exists some powerful loadstone attraction that draws it. Therefore, whether the apple, when it leaves the limb of the tree, is drawn or impelled downward to the nearest point of resistance, is unknown to the students of physics.

Sir James Ross claimed to have discovered the magnetic pole at about seventy-four degrees latitude. This is wrong — the magnetic pole is exactly one-half the distance through the earth's crust. Thus, if the earth's crust is three hundred miles in thickness, which is the distance I estimate it to be, then the magnetic pole is undoubtedly one hundred and fifty miles below the surface of the earth, it matters not where the test is made. And at this particular point one hundred and fifty miles below the surface, gravity ceases, becomes neutralized; and when we pass beyond that point on toward the "inside" surface of the earth, a reverse attraction geometrically increases in power, until the other one hundred and fifty miles of distance is traversed, which would bring us out on the "inside" of the earth.

Thus, if a hole were bored down through

the earth's crust at London, Paris, New York, Chicago, or Los Angeles, a distance of three hundred miles, it would connect the two surfaces. While the inertia and momentum of a weight dropped in from the "outside" surface would carry it far past the magnetic center, yet, before reaching the "inside" surface of the earth it would gradually diminish in speed, after passing the halfway point, finally pause and immediately fall back toward the "outside" surface, and continue thus to oscillate, like the swinging of a pendulum with the power removed, until it would finally rest at the magnetic center, or at that particular point exactly one-half the distance between the "outside" surface and the "inside" surface of the earth.

The gyration of the earth in its daily act of whirling around in its spiral rotation — at a rate greater than one thousand miles every hour, or about seventeen miles per second — makes of it a vast electro-generating body, a huge machine, a mighty prototype of the puny-man-made dynamo, which, at best, is but a feeble imitation of nature's original,

The valleys of this inner Atlantis Continent, bordering the upper waters of the farthest north are in season covered with the most magnificent and luxuriant flowers. Not hundreds and thousands, but millions, of acres, from which the pollen or blossoms are carried far away in almost every direction by the earth's spiral gyrations and the agitation of the wind resulting therefrom, and it is these blossoms or pollen from the vast floral meadows "within" that produce the colored snows of the Arctic regions that have so mystified the northern explorers.[25]

[25 Kane, vol. I, page 44, says: "We passed the 'crimson cliffs' of Sir John Ross in the forenoon of August 5th. The patches of red snow from which they derive their name could be seen clearly at the distance of ten miles from the coast."

La Chambre, in an account of Andree's balloon expedition, on page 144, says: "On the isle of Amsterdam the snow is tinted with red for a considerable distance, and the savants are collecting it to examine it microscopically. It presents, in fact, certain pecu-

liarities; it is thought that it contains very small plants. Scoresby, the famous whaler, had already remarked this."]

Beyond question, this new land "within" is the home, the cradle, of the human race, and viewed from the standpoint of the discoveries made by us, must of necessity have a most important bearing on all physical, paleontological, archaeological, philological and mythological theories of antiquity.

The same idea of going back to the land of mystery — to the very beginning — to the origin of man — is found in Egyptian traditions of the earlier terrestrial regions of the gods, heroes and men, from the historical fragments of Manetho, fully verified by the historical records taken from the more recent excavations of Pompeii as well as the traditions of the North American Indians.

It is now one hour past midnight — the new year of 1908 is here, and this is the third day thereof, and having at last finished the record of my strange travels and adventures I wish given to the world, I am ready, and even longing, for the peaceful rest which I am sure will follow life's trials and vicissitudes. I am old in years, and ripe both with adventures and sorrows, yet rich with the few friends I have cemented to me in my struggles to lead a just and upright life. Like a story that is well-nigh told, my life is ebbing away. The presentiment is strong within me that I shall not live to see the rising of another sun. Thus do I conclude my message. OLAF JANSEN.

PART SEVEN

AUTHOR'S AFTERWORD

I FOUND much difficulty in deciphering and editing the manuscripts of Olaf Jansen. However, I have taken the liberty of reconstructing only a very few expressions, and in doing this have in no way changed the spirit or meaning. Otherwise, the original text has neither been added to nor taken from.

It is impossible for me to express my opinion as to the value or reliability of the wonderful statements made by Olaf Jansen. The description here given of the strange lands and people visited by him, location of cities, the names and directions of rivers, and other information herein combined, conform in every way to the rough drawings given into my custody by this ancient Norseman, which drawings together with the manuscript it is my intention at some later date to give to the Smithsonian Institution, to preserve for the benefit of those interested in the mysteries of the "Farthest North" — the frozen circle of silence. It is certain there are many things in Vedic literature, in ***"Josephus,"*** the ***"Odyssey,"*** the ***"Iliad,"*** Terrien de Lacouperie's ***"Early History of Chinese Civilization,"*** Flammarion's ***"Astronomical Myths,"*** Lenormant's ***"Beginnings of History,"*** Hesiod's ***"Theogony,"*** Sir John de Maundeville's writings, and Sayce's ***"Records of the Past,"*** that, to say the least, are strangely in harmony with the seemingly incredible text found in the yellow manuscript of the old Norseman, Olaf Jansen, and now for the first time given to the world.

THE END

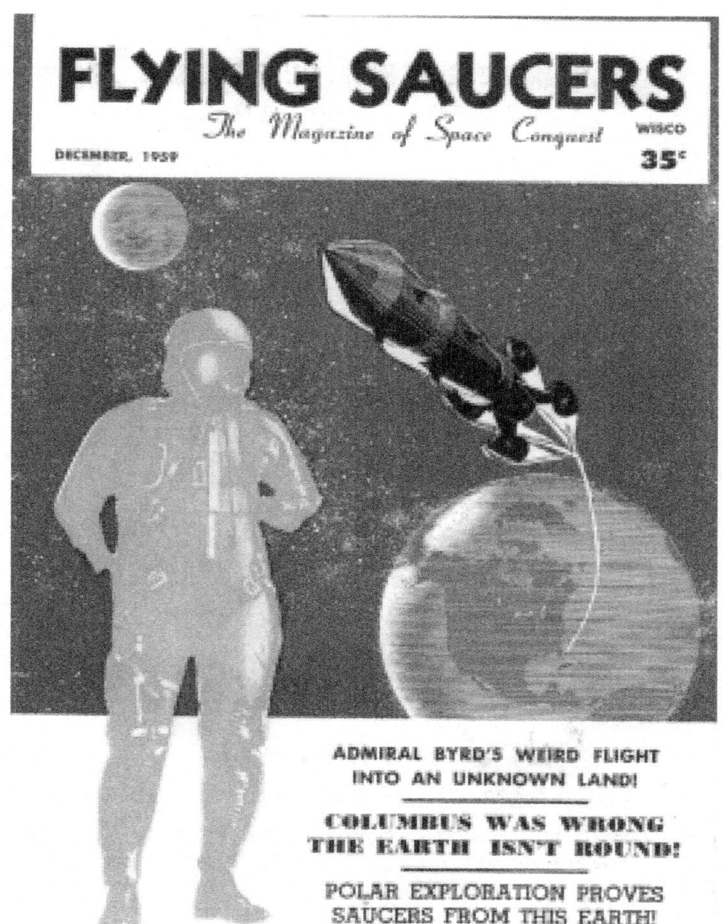
FLYING SAUCERS
The Magazine of Space Conquest
DECEMBER, 1959
WISCO
35¢
ADMIRAL BYRD'S WEIRD FLIGHT INTO AN UNKNOWN LAND!
COLUMBUS WAS WRONG THE EARTH ISN'T ROUND!
POLAR EXPLORATION PROVES SAUCERS FROM THIS EARTH!

Part Eight

Saucers From Earth!

By Ray Palmer

Introduction

THE LATE Ray Palmer started writing science-fiction in the 1930s, and later became editor of Amazing Stozies and other science-fiction magazines in the 1940s. He soon shocked the world when he published the "true tales" of one reader—Richard Shaver—who maintained that he was in contact with beings from the depths of the Earth.

Later on, as editor of his own magazine, ***Flying Saucers***, Palmer shocked the sensibilities of his readers when he proclaimed, in the December, 1959 issue, that the Earth was hollow and could be entered at either the North or South Pole. This is a direct reprint of the astounding revelations he brought to the public.

A Challenge to Secrecy!

Flying Saucers has amassed a large file of evidence which its editors consider unassailable, to prove that the flying saucers are native to the planet Earth; that the govemments of more than one nation (if not all of them) know this to be fact; that a concerted effort is being made to learn all about them, and to explore their native land; that the facts already known are considered so important that they are the world's top secret; that the danger is so great that to offer public proof is to risk widespread panic; that public knowledge would bring public demand for action which would topple governments both helpless and unwilling to comply; that the inherent nature of the flying saucers and their origination area is completely disruptive to political and economic status-quo.

Since the day Kenneth Arnold first brought flying saucers to wide public attention by his famous sighting, one fact has been consistently brought forth by investigators: flying saucers did not originate with that sighting, but have been with humanity for centuries if not thousands of years. Flying Saucers is the popular term for Unidentified Flying Objects (UFO), or Unidentified Aerial Phenomena (UAP). The popular "saucer" shape is only a segment of the phenomena. Properly, the important fact to consider is that intelligently controlled phenomena appear in our atmosphere. Their exact nature is a matter for conjecture, and is quite varied in configuration (to use a favorite Air Force word). It is this fact of antiquity which poses the most important single factor in analyzing the phenomena. At one stroke it eliminates contemporary earth governments as the originators of the mysterious phenomena.

Because of this antiquity, many investigators have turned from the earth to other planets, and to other solar systems. Each planet has its followers in this group of investigators, and such bodies as Venus, Mars and Saturn are favorites with the so-called contactees. We are not at all concerned in this symposium of evidence with the contactee—a phenomenon as "unidentified" as UFO themselves. It may not even be remotely related. However, chief among the advocates of interplanetary origin is Major Donald E. Keyhoe, whose efforts are entirely directed toward collecting evidence that will serve to advance this theory. The interplanetary theorist has a large following, and is perhaps the only theory that will even be considered by scientific men such as astronomers. While it is true that there are many mysteries of an interplanetary nature, linking them with UFO demands a stretching of the evidence, and a great deal of extrapolation. It may be true that there are "configurations" on the Moon, for instance, which are used by Keyhoe to postulate "flying saucers" on that body. Unfortunately (for Keyhoe) this same evidence is used by contactees such as Adamski to support their contentions. Actually, the Moon is remote, in reference to Unidentified Aerial Phenomena, and we must disregard it when we speak of atmospheric phenomena—events which occur within our atmosphere. Since almost all "sightings" are in the atmosphere in nature, the greatest percentage of thinking on them must be limited to the atmosphere.

Because our planet is quite well (but not completely) known, it has been easy for interplanetary theorists to prove that the strange objects are not made by any single government or group of governments on Earth. Such a vast project could not remain secret over so long a period, and also, the matter of antiquity does not allow the phenomena to be fitted into the history of existing governments.

How well-known is the Earth? Is there any area on Earth which can be regarded as a possible origin for the flying saucers? There are two, speaking in major terms, and four, speaking in more minor terminology. The two major areas, in order of importance, are Antarctica and the Arctic. The South Polar continent, and the North Polar area. We speak of the North Polar area because exploration made public to date indicates there is no land, but that it is an ocean, frozen over with ice, under which exploration by submarine is being conducted. The two minor areas are South America's Mato Grosso and Asia's Tibetan Highlands.

Could the flying saucers come from any of these areas? We can largely eliminate the Mato Grosso and the Tibetan Highlands; firstly because of the enormous numbers of the UFO, and secondly because these areas are not entirely unexplored, and can be flown over almost at will. Evidence is lacking in both these areas. Negative evidence, however, does exist in some measure, sufficiently to cause theorists to discard both areas, except in a minor way. At most, either or both Mato Grosso and Tibetan Highland, can be suspected to be "bases" or something on the order of "way stations".

What about the North Pole? Explorers say it is entirely oceanic in nature, covered with ice which sometimes melts in part, and in many areas is quite thin at all times. The depth of the ocean beneath this ice varies from some 24 fathoms to several miles. Flights have been made to and across the North Pole. Submarines, notably Nautilus and Skate, have traveled to the Pole and returned, cmssing from one side to the other (Point Barrow to Spitzbergen). Apparently the sort of base necessary for the UFO mystery in its entirety does not exist in the North Polar regions.

What about the South Pole? Here we have a continent quite as large as North and South America combined, insofar as land mass is concerned. At least one large area (40,000 square miles) is known to experience 100% melting during the summer, and even in winter possesses warm water lakes (from warm springs, geysers, etc). This area is under control of the Russians, who have a permanent base there. Expeditions from both Little America and from the British zone of exploration, have reached the South Pole. Expeditions have also reached the South magnetic Pole. This is a distinction it is necessary to stress, due to the strange fact that the South Magnetic Pole is actually 2300 miles distant from the South Geographic Pole. It is a fact that a tremendous land area exists in the South Pole Continental Area which is unexplored and which constitutes a large blank on the map of the Earth.

Let us consider the North Pole first, and discover what we know about it. What are the facts about the "top" of the Earth?

First, it is surrounded on all sides by known areas of land. Siberia, Spitzbergen, Alaska, Canada, Finland, Norway, Greenland, Iceland. The northern shores of these lands border on the Arctic Ocean, in the virtual center of which both the geographic and magnetic poles exist. These two poles are separated by less than 200 miles, and one of them, the magnetic pole, is known to "wander" somewhat.

The North Pole has been reached by a number of expeditions. The latest we know of are the exploits of the Nautilus and Skate, both atomic submarines which traversed the entire extent of the Arctic Ocean beneath the ice, making the Pole itself (magnetic) a stopping point. On the surface of things, it can be said that the North Polar Area is fairly well explored. In addition to our submarine explorations, the Russians have also traversed the Arctic Ocean. They have even established magnetic "bases", navigational aids which they have planted along Alaskan and Canadian shores, so that rocket-launching atomic bomb submarines can proceed swiftly to a prearranged launching site, and fire rockets on prearranged courses. American submarines have been busily (we hope) moving these navigational aids to new sites which throw off the prearranged calculations, thus making them worthless.

But there is an area of doubt which ***Flying Saucers*** intends to explore, and to present as the first of its bits of evidence which point to what may well be the best kept secret in history. In order to do so, we must go back to 1947. In February of that year, Admiral Richard E. Byrd, the one man who has done the most to make the North Pole a known area, made the following statement: "I'd like to see that land beyond the Pole. That area beyond the Pole is the center of the great Unknown."

Millions of people read his statement in their daily newspapers. And millions thrilled to the Admiral's subsequent flight to the Pole and to a point 1700 miles beyond it. Millions heard the radio broadcast description of that flight, which was also published in the newspapers. Briefly, for the benefit of our readers, we will recount that flight as it progressed. When the plane took off from its Arctic base, it proceeded straight north to the Pole. From that point, it flew on a total of 1700 miles beyond the Pole, and then retraced its course to its Arctic base. As progress was made beyond the Pole point, iceless land and lakes, mountains covered with trees, and even a monstrous animal moving through the underbrush, were observed and reported via radio by the plane's occupants. For almost all of the 1700 miles the plane flew over land, mountains, trees, lakes, rivers.

What land was it? Look at your map. Calculate the distance to the Pole from all the known lands we have previously mentioned. A good portion of them are well within the 1700 mile range. But none of them are within 200 miles of the Pole. Byrd flew over no known land. He himself called it "the great unknown." And great it is, indeed! For after 1700 miles over land, he was forced by gasoline supply limit to return, and he had not yet reached the end of it! He should have been well inside one of the known areas mentioned. He should have been back to "civilization". But he was not. He should have seen nothing but ice-covered ocean, or at the very most, partially open ocean. Instead he was over mountains covered with forests.

Incrediblel The northernmost limit of the timberline is located well down into Alaska, Canada and Siberia. North of that line no tree grows. All around the North Pole, the tree does not grow within 1700 miles of the Pole!

What have we here? We have the well-authenticated flight of Admiral Richard E. Byrd to a land beyond the Pole that he so much wanted to see, because it was the center of the unknown, the center of mystery. Apparently he had his wish gratified to the fullest, yet today, in 1959, nowhere is that mysterious land mentioned. Why? Was that 1947 flight fiction? Did all the newspapers lie? Did the radio from Byrd's plane lie?

No, Admiral Byrd did fly beyond the

Pole.

Beyond?

what did the Admiral mean when he used that word? How is it possible to go "beyond" the Pole? Let us consider for a moment: Let us imagine that we are transported, by some miraculous means, to the exact point of the North magnetic Pole. We arrive there instantaneously, not knowing from which direction we came. And all we know is that we are to proceed from the Pole to Spitzbergen. But where is Spitzbergen? Which way do we go? South, of coursel But which south? All directions from the North Pole are south!

This is actually a simple navigational problem. All expeditions to the Pole, whether flown, or by submarine, or on foot, have been faced with this problem. Either they must retrace their steps, or discover which southerly direction is the correct one to their destination, whatever it has been determined to be. The problem is solved by making a turn, in any direction, and proceeding approximately 20 miles. Then we stop, shoot the stars, correlate with our compass reading (which no longer points straight down, but toward the North Magnetic Pole), and plot our course on the map. Then it is a simple matter to proceed to Spitzbergen by going south.

Admiral Byrd did not follow this traditional navigational procedure: when he reached the Pole, he continued on for 1700 miles. To all intents and purposes, he continued on a northerly course, after crossing the Pole. And weirdly, it stands on the record that he succeeded, for he did see that "land beyond the Pole" which to this day, if we are to scan the records of newspapers, book, radio, television and word of mouth, has never been revisitedl

That land, on today's maps, cannot exist. But since it does, we can only conclude that today's maps are incorrect, incomplete, and do not present a true picture of the northern hemisphere!

Having thus located a great land mass in the North, not on any map today, a land which is the center of the great unknown, which can only be construed to imply that the 1700 mile extent traversed by Byrd is only a portion of it, let us go to the south Pole and see what we can learn about it.

On April 5, 1955, the U.S. Navy announced an expedition to the South Pole. It was to be headed by Admiral Richard E. Byrd. It consisted of five ships, fourteen airplanes, special tractors, and a complement of 1393 men. The stated purpose of the expedition was as follows: "To construct a satellite base at the South Pole."

In San Francisco, on the eve of his departure, Admiral Byrd delivered a radio address in which he stated: "This is the most important expedition in the history of the world."

Let us pause a moment and pretend we are rocket men, primarily the scientis trocket-men who are engaged in launching satellites. Our task is a troublesome one. Many failures result. Our work is a tremendously difficult task and sometimes important rocket shoots are delayed for days by weather. Our base is a gigantic one, here at Cape Canaveral. The logistics problem is enormous. The rockets themselves weigh hundreds of tons. To be asked to set up such a satellite base at the South Pole would cause us to stare in utter amazement at the official making the request. We would waste no time in informing him that he hasten immediately to his psychiatrist and retire from active service, for he has indeed "gone off his rocker". In short, a satellite base at the tip of South America in plain words, is totally ridiculous. Even a satellite tracking station at the South Pole is nothing short of idiotic. For tracking purposes, a base at the tip of South America is entirely adequate. Or on a series of ships anchored about the Antarctic Circle.

This, then, cannot be a satellite base. It must be something else. On January 13, 1956, we learn what it really is. On that date the U.S. Navy flies to a point 2300 miles beyond the South Pole. The entire distance is accomplished over land.

Once again, look at your map. Unlike the North Polar Sea, the South Polar Continent is entirely surrounded by water. And in all cases, no matter what direction you proceed from the South Pole, you pass from the continental area to a known oceanic area.

You proceed hundreds of miles over water to reach a distance of 2300 miles.

Once again we have penetrated an unknown and mysterious land which does not appear on today's maps. And once again, we find no further announcement beyond the initial announcement of the achievement.

And strangest of all, we find the world's millions absorbing the announcements, and registering a complete blank insofar as curiosity is concerned. Nobody, hearing the announcements, or reading of them in the newspaper, bothers to get a map and check the facts! Or if they do, they only shake their heads in puzzlement, and then shrug their shoulders. If Admiral Byrd is not bothered with the apparent inconsistencies, why should they be?

Here, then, are the facts. At both poles exist unknown and vast land areas, not in the least uninhabitable, extending for distances which can only be called tremendous, because they encompass an area bigger than any known continental area! The North Polar Mystery Land seen by Byrd and his crew is at least 1700 miles across its traversed direction, and cannot be conceived to be merely a narrow strip, as the factor of coincidence in flying precisely along its longest extent is improbable. It is a land area perhaps as large as the entire United States! The land area at the South Pole, considering that the flight began 400 miles west of the Pole, and thus covers a continuous land area of 2700 miles in one direction, means a land area possibly as big as North America in addition to the known extent of the South Polar Continent, which is located north of the Pole whereas the 2300-mile land traversed by the Navy plane is "beyond" the Pole. Once more the same condition of navigation exists: progress was made to the Pole and then straight on beyond it, with the one difference that the South Geographic Pole is located 2300 miles away from the South Magnetic Pole, and it is not necessary to perform the navigational maneuver described previously. if navigating from the South magnetic Pole, the procedure is again necessary, with differences due to the greater angle of inclination to the stars, and the possibility of navigation entirely by the stars rather than with the aid of a compass.

Let's stop here and make a statement that logically follows: the flying saucers could come from these two unknown lands "beyond the Poles". It is the opinion of the editors of ***Flying Saucers*** that the existence of these lands cannot be disproved by anyone, considering. the facts of the two expeditions which we have outlined. These facts can be checked by anyone. You have merely to read the newspapers of the day. If there is anyone who can satisfactorily explain away these two expeditions, and the statements of Admiral Richard E. Byrd concerning them, ***Flying Saucers*** will give him every inch of space necessary to complete his explanation.

Just for the record, let's present the actual announcement carried by press and radio on February 5, 1956: "On January 13, members of the United States expedition accomplished a flight of 2700 miles from the base at McMurado Sound which is 400 miles west of the South Pole, and penetrated a land extent of 2300 miles beyond the Pole."

And on March 13, Admiral Byrd reported, upon his return from the South Pole: "The present expedition has opened up a vast new land."

Finally, in 1957, before his death, he reported it as: "That enchanted continent in the sky, land of everlasting mystery!" Which statement remains to your editors as the most mysterious of all, and almost inexplicable. "Enchanted continent in the sky..." Everlasting mystery, indeed!

Considering all this, is there any wonder that all the nations of the world have suddenly found the South Polar region (particularly), because of its known land area and the North Pole region so intensely interesting and important, and have launched explorations on a scale truly tremendous in scope?

And was it because of Admiral Byrd's weird flight into an unknown Polar land in 1947 that the International Geophysical Year was conceived in that year, and finally brought to fruition ten years later, and is actually still going on? Did his flight make it suddenly imperative to discover the real nature of this planet we live on, and solve the tremendous mysteries that unexpectedly confronted us?

If you have followed us thus far, it may be that you have gone to your map or your globe and have tried to fit these mysterious lands onto the planet, and have come up with a snort and said: "These bits of evidence are all very well, but the fact remains there is nowhere physically to place these land masses. Since the space to do so is lacking, there exists a fundamental impossibility which cannot be overcome." Good boy! Don't give up your guns. Insist that we overcome this fundamental impossibility, and support our original evidence in not a few ways, but in hundreds....

The question that most logically follows the two instances of exploration which we have outlined is whether or not other Polar Expeditions have encountered similar and confirming conditions. In order to answer this question, it will be necessary to examine the records of all North and South Pole explorations from the very first of which modem man has any knowledge. As a subsubject, it might be interesting later on to go into legend and mythology for still further bits of confirmation, but we are concerned now only with presenting provable facts. In the presentation of these facts, we intend to draw no conclusion. They should become obvious to the reader without prompting.

To those of our readers so inclined, there must be a great deal of interest on their part. In the historically famous debate on which both, or neither, Cook or Perry actually reached the North Pole. In the years following these expeditions, much debate went on, and even today arguments rage. Briefly, let's outline the claims of both men.

Dr. Frederick A. Cook said he reached the Pole on April 21, 1908. His announcement was followed by a few days by one from Rear Admiral Robert E. Peary that he had reached the Pole on April 6, 1909. Both men hurled accusations against the other, Cook even saying that Peary had appropriated some of his stores cached against his return from the Pole. Cook in his turn failed to supply notes he said he had kept of his trip, and thereby cast doubt an his own story. The reader who is interested in the whole story should visit his library and read up on the controversy.

Although Cook claims to have been the first to reach the Pole we will take Pearys claim, which has been universally recognized, and examine it. Cook's claim was discredited on one basis because the sun's altitude was so low that observations of it as proof of position were worthless. It should be noted that Peary also reached the Pole in April, 15 days earlier in the season, and therefore under even more adverse solar observations conditions. His calculations therefore are more suspect than Cook's. Cook, it was said, had no witnesses other than Eskimos; the same is true of Peary. Peary, however, lacked witnesses through choice, having ordered his white companions to remain behind, while he went on alone with one Eskimo companion to the Pole. Cook was doubted in his claim that he averaged 15 miles a day. Peary claimed to have made over 20. Undoubtedly the argument will never be settled. However, there is the factor regarding Peary's dash to the Pole, which, in our opinion, is quite remarkable. This factor lies in the fantastic speed with which he made his trip.

When Peary neared the 88th parallel, he decided to attempt the final dash to the Pole in five days. He made 25 miles the first day; 20 on the second; 20 on the third; 25 on the fourth; 40 on the fifth. His five-day average was 26 miles. On the return trip he traveled a total of 153 miles in two days, including a halt 5 miles from the Pole to take a sounding of the ocean depth. This is an average of 76 1/2 miles per day. His actual traveling time was approximately 19 hours per day. This is a walking speed of 4 miles per hour. Can a man walk that fast under the incredible conditions of the North Pole area, an ice-terrain described by the men of the atomic submarine Skate as fantastically jumbled and jagged? And yet, further south, with presumably better going, he was able to average only 20 miles per day.

We stress the distances only because

the ones nearest the Pole are weirdly impossible. Only if Peary was reporting honestly would we have included such contradictory calculations which he must have known would discredit his story. Therefore we can assume that he did report honestly, and that we have a speed of travel which projects into the same mysterious area in the same "unfittable" manner as a whole vast continent fits into a space that is totally lacking. When traveling over a land whose dimensions are fantastically "expanded," will we not also travel at an equally fantastically "expanded" speed? It will be well to remember that these speeds were calculated by astronomical observation, because the astronomical basis of these calculations will be taken up later in presentation of evidence.

To those who will study up on the subject of Polar Exploration, it will soon become evident that the feature most agreed upon by all North Polar explorers is that the area is oceanic, covered by water, and that it is variously frozen over or partially open, depending on the time of year. One peculiarity which many explorers remark upon, however, is that paradoxically, the open water exists in greater measure at the nearer reaches of the Pole. In fact, some explorers found it very hot going at times, and were forced to shed their Arctic clothing; there even being one record of an encounter with naked Eskimos. Yet, with all this confirmed oceanic area, we have the contradiction of Admiral Byrd's flight being almost entirely over land, mountains covered with trees, interspersed with lakes and streams.

One of the reports from Byrd's expedition was the sighting of a huge animal with dark fur. Are there such animals, or traces of them, in the Arctic? Beginning in Siberia, along the Lena river, there lie exposed on the soil, and buried within it, the bones and tusks of literally millions of mammoths and mastodons. The consensus of scientific opinion is that these are prehistoric remains, and that the mammoth existed some 20,000 years ago, and was wiped out in the unknown catastrophe we now call the last Ice Age. In 1799, a fisherman named Schumachoff, living in Tongoose (Siberia), discovered a complete mammoth frozen in a clear block of ice. Hacking it free, he despoiled it of its huge tusks and left the carcass of fresh meat be be devoured by wolves. Later an expedition set out to examine it, and today its skeleton may still be seen in the Museum of Natural History in Petrograd (then St. Petersburg).

Early in the century, approximately 1910, a very scientific meal was served in Petrograd. It consisted of wheat from the Egyptian tombs, preserved foods from Pompeii and Herculaneum, mammoth meat from Siberia, and other interesting and ancient viands. The mammoth meat was fresh, and the mammoth from which it had been taken still had undigested food in its stomach, this undigested food consisting of young shocks of fir and pine and young fir cones. According to the scientists, this mammoth was one of the millions slain instantly in a gigantic catastrophe 20,000 years ago, in a habitat then tropical, in which the vegetation was fern and tropical in nature. Yet, in the stomach of this mammoth is found the sparse food of a subArctic area such as much of Alaska or Northern Canada is today. There is good reason to

cast doubt upon the tropic origin of the mammoth, and its sudden demise. And if the demise was not sudden, then the presence of indigested food (not digested even by so much as minutes exposure to stomach acids) in the stomach of the mammoth is unexplainable. True the death must have been sudden, but it was not of tropic locale. If not tropic, then the Ice Age onset is not the cause of death. The cause of death, then, is Arctic in nature, and could have occurred any time. But since the Ice Age, there have been no mammoths in the known world. Unless they exist in the mysterious land beyond the Pole, where one of them was actually seen alive by members of the Byrd expedition. Others who dined on mammoth meat were James Oliver Curwood and Gabrielle DAnnunzio, who gave a banquet at the Hotel Carlton in Paris.

We have taken the mammoth as a rather sensational modern evidence of Byrd's mysterious land, but there are many lesser proofs that an unknown originating point exists somewhere in the northern reaches. We will merely list a few, suggesting that the reader, in examining the records of polar explorers for the past two centuries, will find evidences of both fauna and flora impossible to reconcile with the known areas of land mentioned early in this presentation of facts, those areas surrounding the

Polar Area on your present-day maps.

The musk-ox, contrary to expectations, migrates north in the wintertime. Repeatedly, Arctic explorers have observed bear heading north into an area where there is no food for them. Foxes also are found north of the 90th parallel, heading north, obviously well-fed. Without exception, Arctic explorers agree that the further north one goes, the warmer it gets. Invariably, a north wind brings warmer weather. Coniferous trees drift ashore, from out of the north. Butterflies and bees are found in the far north, but never hundreds miles further south; not until Canadian and Alaskan climate conducive to such insect life are reached. Unknown varieties of flowers are found. Birds resembling snipe, but unlike any known species of bird, come out of the north, and return there. Hare are plentiful in an area where no vegetation ever grows, but where vegetation appears as drifting debris from the northern open waters. Eskimo tribes, migrating northward, have left unmistakable traces of their migration in their temporary camps, always advancing northward. Southern Eskimos themselves speak of tribes that live in the far north. The Ross gull, common at Point Barrow, migrates in October toward the north. Only Admiral Byrd's "mystery land" can account for these inexplicable facts and migrations.

The Scandinavian legend of a wonderful land far to the North called "Ultima Thule" (commonly confused today with Greenland) is significant when studied in detail, because of its remarkable resemblance to the kind of land seen by Byrd, and its remarkable far north location. To assume that Ultima Thule is Greenland is to come face to face with the contradiction of the Greenland Ice Cap, which fill the entire Greenland basin to a depth of 10,000 feet. A green, fertile land in this location places itself so deep in antiquity that it postulates an overturn of the Earth, and a new North Pole area (see National Geographic's exploration of the Greenland Ice Cap and its possible significance).

Is Admiral Byrd's land of mystery, center of the great unknown, the same as the Ultima Thule of the Scandinavian legends?

There are mysteries concerning the

Antarctic also. Perhaps the greatest is a highly technical one of biology itself; for on the New Zealand and South American land masses are identical fauna and flora which could not have migrated from one to the other, but rather are believed to have come from a common motherland. That motherland is believed to be the Antarctic Continent. But on a more "popular" level is the case of the sailing vessel Gladys captained by E.B. Hatfield, in 1893. The ship was completely surrounded by icebergs at 43 degrees south and 33 degrees west and finally escaped its entrapment at 40 degrees south and 30 degrees west. At this latitude an iceberg was observed which bore a large quantity of sand and earth, and which revealed a beaten track a place of refuge formed in a sheltered nook, and the bodies of five dead men who lay on different parts of the berg. Bad weather prevented any attempts at further investigation.

Bear in mind that it is a unanimous consensus of opinion among scientists that the one thing peculiar to the Antarctic is that there are no human tribes living upon it. But this consensus must be wrong, because investigation showed that no vessel was lost in the Antarctic at that time, so that these dead men could not have been shipwrecked sailors. Even today, with Antarctic exploration at its height, the lack of human life on that bleak continent is agreed upon. Could it be that these men who died on that berg came from "that mysterious land beyond the South Pole" discovered by the Byrd expedition? Had they ventured out of their warm, habitable land and lost their way along the ice shelf, finally to be drifted to their deaths at sea on a portion of it, broken away to become an iceberg while they were on it?

Most recent evidence that there is something strange about the Poles of Earth comes in the launching of Polar orbit satellites. The first six of these rockets launched by the United States from the California coast were full of disappointments and surprises. The first two, although perfect launchings, seemed to go wrong at the last minute, and although presumed to be in orbit, failed to show up on the first complete pass around the Earth. Technically speaking, they should have gone into orbit but they did not. Something happened, and the location of this something was the Polar area. The next two rockets fired did achieve orbits. This was done by "elevating sights", so to speak and trying for a higher orbit, with a large degree of eccentricity, that is, a high point of orbit above the poles and a low point of orbit at equatorial areas. It was admitted that this eccentric orbit would produce a short-lived orbit, but it would also give the advantage of readings at widely varied heights above the Earth. Especially interesting was the readings expected above the Poles, because of the discovery of the radiation ring that surrounds the Earth like a huge doughnut, with openings at both Poles. Scientists were very anxious to map this area of low radiation, because it offered a hope of an escape breach for future space travelers who faced almost certain death from radiation while passing through the forbidding belt discovered around the equatorial and temperate areas of the Earth.

The next two satellites bore nose cones similar to those in which a future astronaut would be sent into orbit. In each one was a powerful radio transmitter, which was possible because the cone was the size of an automobile, and carried heavy batteries. Also included were powerful lights which could be illuminated at the proper time. The technique of releasing this cone from the satellite was to drop it by a radio-triggered device somewhere above Alaska. Once dropped, the cone lost altitude and proceeded around the Earth for one more revolution on its orbit. Having come over the Pole, it was then low enough (calculated the rocket men) to drop into the atmosphere over Hawaii, where a parachute would lower it slowly to the Earth's surface, and there huge planes awaited, rigged to

"fish for" the descending cone, and take it to the plane before it dropped into the ocean and thus retrieve its important contents intact, without damage of crash landing.

On both occasions the following happened: The powerful radio signals were not heard at all. The lights were not seen at all. Radar, with a range at least 500 miles detected absolutely nothing. Each "pick-up" was a complete failure because there was nothing to pick up.

The explanation of the radio failure was advanced as "freezing" of the batteries so that the radio failed to work No explanation was given for the failure of lights, or of radar detection. That the batteries froze is a strange explanation, considering that similar batteries in other satellites, orbiting for months, and even years, have never frozen. Failure might be admitted in one case, but total failure in both instances bears the aura of improbability.

Each launching was perfect, orbits finely determined as to exact distance, speed, etc. were achieved, and constantly tracked.

Yet, when the final deed is done, and the cone is detached successfully according to monitoring devices signaling the detachment, everything goes wrong and the result is complete and inexplicable disappearance of the cone. True, the statement is made that there is only a 1000 to 1 chance of success, and thus two failures are not unreasonable. But the failures are not to be complete ones. By failure is meant the successful final "pick-up" of the cone by the aircraft. Not complete disappearance! At least radio signals will be received, lights will be seen, radar will spot the descending cone.

Can it be that the reason the descending cone does not come over the Pole on that last low pass is because the Polar Area is mysterious in extent, not in the area calculated by the rocket men, and therefore not taken into consideration? Can it be that the nose cone fell to Earth inside that "land of mystery" discovered by Admiral Byrd? Where else could they have gone? If the Earth at the Poles is as given on today's maps, could four successive "low-level" launchings give the same inexplicable result—unreasonable disappearance?

If there is 1700 (or more) miles of land extent in addition to the area bounded by longitudes and latitudes on a sphere existing in the Axctic, it follows that the recorded disappearances are not inexplicable, but certain to occur! Naturally a rocket cone figured to traverse a certain distance (in these cases approximately 33,000 miles) will not land at a predetermined point if the distance to be traveled is greater by 1700 miles. Our radar will fail to find our cone, and our eyes will see no lights. But why will our radio fail to send its signals to us? Is it because that "land of mystery" is of an "intervening" nature? Radio waves will not go through the Earth, of course. If solid substance intervenes, then we can understand why radio waves do not penetrate it. But what kind of a land configuration can it be that "intervenes" in this way? Why don't we have the "skip and bounce" effect from the stratosphere, which presumably exists over Byrd's "land of mystery" as well as over the lands on the map?

Since the mapped area of the spherical

Earth does not allow sufficient room in which to place our two mystery lands, can it be that the Earth is of a different shape, one that allows us to place these lands on that portion of it which does not come under the category of "spherical"? To many readers this will bring a snort and a humorous smile. They will say that we are bringing up the old saw of the Earth not being round. Columbus, they will say, finally proved that to the Earth's peoples, and Magellan actually did sail completely around the Earth by sailing in one direction until he had come back to his starting point. Also, anyone can go out on the night of a Lunar Eclipse, and see the round shadow of the Earth cross the face of the Moon. Seeing is believing, they will say—and just try to get around that!

It is true that seeing is believing, for most people. But the most informed optical scientist will not hold that popular view. He will point out that the human eye, like the telescope, is a lens. And the proved property of any lens is that it tends to make everything look round. No matter what we look at, distance converts the lines of the observed object from straight, or angular, or crooked, to perfectly circular one. This is a familiar phenomenon to aviators, who know that from the air, no house has a square chimney; they are all round. Any aircraft carrier pilot will tell you that as he brings in his jet at a great height, his carrier looks like a round dot beneath him, and as he descends, it becomes a rectangle again. Anyone who has gone through a railroad tunnel, riding on the rear platform, will testify that the tunnel opening, if square, will gradually grow round as the train proceeds into the tunnel. Optical illusions, they are called. Any camera expert will tell you that the film records distant or extremely small objects as round dots, and that great magnification is necessary to resolve this roundness, and beyond a certain limit (that of the "grain" of the emulsion itself it is impossible to resolve this roundness.

The scientific fact is that were the Moon actually square, at a distance of 240,000 miles our eye, our telescope, our camera would tell us it is round! No matter what shape it is, we would see it only as round.

Actually, we cannot prove that the Moon is round; nor the Earth.

Thus, the arguments for a perfectly round Earth are not based on fact, only on assumption. This assumption is based on a brand of astronomy no longer acceptable to the scientist. Today the nebular theory of formation of planets, suns, even galaxies, is looked upon favorably. The condensation of nebula into stars and planets is accomplished by whirling motion. The whirling motion more often produces the "spindle" shape, round at the "equator", and projecting at the "pole"; or the "doughnut" shape, with flattened poles and holes through the middle. Since the Earth so formed, it may well be that it is either shape. We would not be aware of it by optical evidence, as we have shown.

On the one hand, the "spindle" shape possesses many specific arguments against it, and is the least reasonable. Astronomical bearings taken anywhere on the "spindle" portion would begin to show telltale evidence of the existence of the "spindle" shape. And they would be the reverse of factual sightings and bearings taken by Polar explorers. Actually, the bearings taken point to the "doughnuf shape.

Let us go back to Admiral Perry: his astounding rate of travel on his return from the Pole. If he were traveling over the inner lip of a "doughnut" shape, his bearings would indicate a great distance traveled, due to the fore-shortened horizon, and the "expanded" angle used in making his trigonometrical calculations. Actually he would be traveling the same distance each day, and the drop in speed would be entirely compatible with the bearing observations taken with a constantly lengthening horizon.

Rocket scientists have made much of the discovery of the Van Allen Belt, which is a belt of radiation surrounding the Earth. The reader is invited to read about it in Sciendfic American, and especially note the drawings of its shape, which are precisely a vast "doughnut", with the spherical Earth pictured at its center, in the "hole" of the doughnut. What if the Earth is not spherical, but actually doughnut shaped, exactly as its surrounding Van Allen Belt? Whatever makes the belt thusly shaped, might it not also be responsible for shaping the Earth similarly?

The evidence is extremely strong, and amazingly prolific in scope and extent, that the Earth actually is shaped in this fashion. And if it is hollow, then we no longer need look for the saucers from outer space, but rather from 'inner space"! And judging from the evidences, the interior is extremely habitable! Vegetation in abundance is there; animals abound; the "extinct" mammoth still lives! Byrd flew 1700 miles over the inner edge of the "doughnut hole", and the Navy flew 2300 miles over the opposite inner edge. Both flights went a partial way into the inner Earth. And if this is all true, then no doubt extended flights to 10,000 miles and beyond have been made since 1957 into this hollow Earth, for we have the planes with the range to do it! If the government knew the significance of the Byrd Navy flights, it would certainly not neglect to explore further!

Aime Aachel, in his "straight line" theory, proved that most of the "flight patterns" of the flying saucers are on a north-south course, which is exactly what would be true if the origin of the saucers is Polar.

In the opinion of the editors of ***Flying Saucers*** this Polar origin of the flying saucers will now have to be factually disproved. It is completely necessary that this be done; more than a simple denial is necessary. Any denial must be accompanied with positive proof. ***Flying Saucers*** suggests that such proof cannot be provided. And until such proof is provided, ***Flying Saucers*** takes the stand that all saucer groups should study the matter from the hollow Earth viewpoint, amass all confirmatory evidence available in the last two centuries, and search diligently for any contrary evidence. Now that we have tracked the saucers to the most logical origin (the one we have consistently insisted must exist because of the insurmountable obstacle of interstellar origin which demands factors almost beyond imagination), that the saucers come from our own Earth, it must be proved or disproved, one way or the other.

Why? Because if the interior of the Earth is populated by a highly scientific and advanced race, we must make profitable contact with them; and if they are mighty in their science, which includes the science of war, we must not make enemies of them; and if it is the intent of our governments to regard the interior of

Earth as "virgin territory", and comparable to the "Indian Territory" of North America when the settlers came over to take it away from its rightful owners, it is the right of the people to know that intent, and to express their desire in the matter.

The Flying Saucer has become the most important single fact in history. The answer to the questions raised in this article must be answered. Admiral Byrd has discovered a new and mysterious land, the center of the great unknown, and the most important discovery of all time. We have it from his own lips, from a man whose integrity has always been unimpeachable, and whose mind was one of the most brilliant of modem times.

Let those who wish to call him a liar step

forward and prove their claim!

Flying saucers come from this Earth!

Part Nine

Secrets of the Subterranean Cities

By The World Ascension Network

THE World Ascension Network (360 Montezuma, Suite 221, Santa Fe, NM 87501) promotes the work of Sharula, princess of the underground city beneath Mt Shasta. Here is the information they provided us on this famous entrance to the Inner Earth.

If you're reading this, chances are you haven't attended a meeting of the meeting of the Flat Earth Society lately. Since you know the Earth is round, consider the possibility that there is something inside of it. Not a sea of molten lava, but a network of polite subterraneans who have been waiting for the surface folk to get a clue. In one of our issues, we introduced you to the wonders of a world within a world. Following in the footsteps of Plato, Homer and Jules Verne— all believers in subterranean culture—we gave an overview of the social structure of the Agartha Network. We told of Admiral Byrd's wing camera documentation of the "holes at the poles," and of the US. government's elaborate expeditions and attempts to make contact. Back by popular demand, we are pleased to bring you a further unveiling of life in the subterranean cities.

Recently, America watched Stephen Speilberg's TV pilot, a remake" of Verne's *"Journey to the Center of the Earth."* A maverick team of scientists aboard their meltproof ship, enter the inner Earth through a bubbling volcano. When things cool off, they find themselves exploring a vast and sunny inner landscape ... a magical and inviting world with ample room to fly.

Their adventure resembles the real life account of a Norwegian sailor named Olaf Jansen. His story, set in the 1800's, is told in Willis Emerson's biography entitled The Smoky God [which forms the first portion of this book-Editor]. Olaf's little sloop drifted so far north by storm, that he actually sailed into a polar entrance, and lived for two years with one of the colonies of the Agartha Network, called "Shamballa the Lesser". He describes his hosts as those "of the central seat of government for the inner continent ... measuring a full 12 feet in height ... extending courtesies and showing kindness ... laughing heartily when they had to improvise chairs for my father and I to sit in." Olaf tells of a "smoky" inner sun, a world comprised of three fourths land and one fourth water.

The Agartha Network

Think of Shamballa the Lessor as the United Nations of over 100 subterranean cities that form the Agartha Network. It is indeed the seat of government for the inner world. While Shamballa the Lessor is an inner continent, its satellite colonies are smaller enclosed ecosystems located just beneath the Earth's crust or discreetly within mountains. All cities in the Agartha Network are physical, and are of the light, meaning that they are benevolent spiritually based societies who follow the Christic teachings of the order of Meichizedek. Quite simply, they continue in the tradition of the great mystery schools of the surface, honoring such beings as Jesus/Sananda, Buddha, Isis and Osiris ... all of the Ascended masters that we of the surface know and love, in addition to spiritual teachers of their own longstanding heritage.

Why did they choose to live underground? Consider the magnitude of the geological Earth changes that have swept the surface over the past 100,000 years. Consider the lengthy Atlantean Lemurian war, and the power of thermo-nuclear weaponry that eventually sank and destroyed these two highly advanced civilizations. The Sahara, the Gobi, the Australian outback, and the deserts of the U.S., are but a few examples of the devastation that resulted. The sub-cities were created as refuges for the people, and as safe havens for sacred records, teachings and technologies that were cherished by these ancient cultures.

Capitol Cities

POSID: Primary Atlantean outpost, located beneath the Mato Grosso plains region of Brazil. Population: 1.3 million.

SHONSHE: Refuge of the Uighur culture, a branch of the Lemurians who chose to form their own colonies 50,000 years ago. Entrance is guarded by a Himalayan lamasary. Population $^3/_4$ million.

RAMA: Remnant of the surface city of Rama, India located near Jaipur. Inhabitants are known for their classic Hindu features. Population 1 million.

SHINGWA: Remnant of the northern migration of the Uighurs. Located on the border of Mongolia and China. Population $^3/_4$ million.

TELOS: Primary Lemurian outpost located within Mt. Shasta, with a small secondary city in Mt. Lassen, California, US. Telos translated means "communication with Spirit". Population 1.5 million.

Spotlight on Telos

Inquiring minds want to know how over

a million people can make their home inside of Mt. Shasta.

While we're stretching our imaginations, our neighbors the Japanese have already blueprinted underground cities in an answer to their surface area problem. Subcity habitation has, for thousands of years, been a natural vehicle for human evolution. Now, here is a peek at a well thought out ecosystem.

The dimensions of this domed city are approximately 1.5 miles wide by 2 miles deep. Telos is comprised of 5 levels.

Level 1: This top level is the center of commerce, education and administration. The pyramid shaped temple is the central structure and has a capacity of 50,000. Surrounding it are government buildings, the equivalent of a courthouse that promotes an enlightened judicial system, halls of records, arts and entertainment facilities, a hotel for visiting foreign emissaries, a palace which houses the "Ra and Rana Mu" (the reigning King and Queen of the royal Lemurian lineage whom are Ascended Masters),a communications tower, a spaceport, schools, food and clothing dispatches, and most residences.

Level 2: A manufacturing center as well as a residential level. Houses are circular in shape, and dust free because of it. Like surface living, housing for singles, couples and extended families is the norm.

Level 3: Hydroponic gardens. Highly advanced hydroponic technology feeds the entire city with some to spare for inter-city commerce. All crops yield larger and tastier fiuits, veggies and soy products that make for a varied and fun diet for Telosians. Now completely vegetarian, the Agartha Cities have taken meat substitutes to new heights.

Level 4: More hydroponic gardens, more manufacturing, some natural park areas.

Level 5: The nature level. Set about a mile beneath surface ground level, this area is a large natural environment. It serves as a habitat for a wide variety of animals, including those many extinct on the surface. All species have been bred in a non-violent atmosphere, and those that might be camivorous on the surface, now enjoy soy steaks, and human interaction. Here you can romp with a Saber Tooth Tiger with wild abandon. Together with the other plant levels, enough oxygen is produced to sustain the biosphere.

LANGUAGE: While dialects vary from city to city, "Solara Maru," translated as the "Solar Language," is commonly spoken. This is the root language for our sacred languages such as Sanskrit and Hebrew.

GOVERNMENT: A Council of Twelve, six men and six women, together with the Ra and Rana Mu, do collective problem solving and serve as guides and guardians of the people. Positions of royalty, such as are held by the Ra and Rana Mu are regarded as ones of responsibility in upholding God's divine plan. The High Priest, an Ascended Master named Adama, is also an official representative.

COMPUTERS: The Agarthean computer system is amino-acid based, and serves a vast array of functions. All of the sub-cities are linked by this highly spiritualized information network. The system monitors intercity and galactic communication, while simultaneously serving the needs of the individual at home. It can, for instance, report your body's vitamin or mineral deficiencies, or when necessary, convey pertinent information from the akashic records for personal growth.

MONEY: Non-existent. All inhabitants' basic needs are taken care of. Luxuries are exchanged via a sophisticated barter system.

TRANSPORTATION: Moving sidewalks, inter-level elevators, and electromagnetic sleds resembling our snow mobiles within the city. For travel between cities, residents take "the Tube," an electromagnetic subway system capable of speeds up to 3,000 mph. Yes, Agartheans are well versed in inter-galactic etiquette, and are members of the Confederation of Planets. Space travel has been perfected, as has the ability for interdimensional shifts that render these ships undetectable.

ENTERTAINMENT: Theatre, concerts, and a wide variety of the arts. Also, for you

Trekkies, the Holodecks. Program your favorite movie or chapter in Earth history, and become a part of it!

CHILDBIRTH: A painless three months, not nine. A very sacred process whereby upon conception, a woman will go to the temple for three days, immediately welcoming the child with beautiful music, thoughts and imagery. Water birthing in the company of both parents is standard.

HEIGHT: Due to cultural differences, average heights of subterranean citizens vary. Generally 6'5" to 7'5" in Telos while nearly 12'in Shamballa the Lessor.

AGE: Unlimited. Death by degeneration is simply not a reality in Telos. Most Agartheans, choose to look an age between 30 and 40, and stay there, while technically they may be thousands of years old. By not believing in death, this society is not limited by it. Upon completing a desired experience, one can disincarnate at will.

ASCENSION: Absolutely, and much easier and more common than on the surface. Ascension is the ultimate goal of temple training.

Why have they stayed underground all this time? In part because the Agartheans have learned the futility of war and violence, and are patiently waiting for us to draw the same conclusion. They are such gentle folk, that even our judgmental thoughts are physically harmful to them. Secrecy has been their protection. Until now, the truth of their existence has been veiled by Spirit.

When can we visit? Our entrance to the sub-cities depends on the purity of our intentions, and our capacity to think positively. A warm welcome from both worlds is the ideal, and must be expressed by more than just the lightworking community.

Currently, a few hundred brave subterraneans are working on the surface. In order to blend with the masses, they have undergone temporary cellular change, so that physically, they don't tower above the rest of us. They may be recognized by their gentle, sensitive nature, and somewhat mysterious accent. We wish to introduce you to a very special one of them.

Her name is Princess Sharula Aurora Dux. The daughter of the Ra and Rana Mu of Telos, Sharula has been officially appointed Ambassador to the surface world by the Agartha Network. She is 267 years old, and looks 30. All of the above is courtesy of her first hand experience. Sharula, currently known to thousands, shall soon be known to millions.

The purpose of her Ambassadorship is to prepare the way for the merging of the two worlds ... to bring the ideas, the information and the new archetypes that will help unite our planet. Sharula has come to present a blueprint for peaceful change to those who will listen. Now, the Agartheans have reached a point where they cannot progress spiritually unless this merger takes place. In essence, we are one planet ascending, nothalf a planet. It is God's will that we take the next step together. The sooner we invite this unity, the sooner the magic will unfold. The Hierarchy has made the emergence of the subterranean cities a priority project. They are asking us to do our part in welcoming our brethren. The timing depends very much upon our receptivity and our graciousness. A successful merger is estimated within the next 10 to 20 years. Beloved, there is nothing to fear, and everything to gain. The gifts the Agartheans bring are many. The secret of immortality is also your birthright. The freedom to live in abundance is also your birthright You haven't lived until you've tasted a hydroponic tomato, and by all means, a little fun on the Holodeck should be had by all.

SHARULA

Introducing the Woman from Telos, the City Beneath Mount Shasta—Sharula

The following interview with Sharula took place on July 23, 1990, and is reprinted from ***Insights For Positive Living***. She shares with us some wonderful information about the Atlantean and Lemurian cities that exist beneath the earth's surface.

She speaks from her home, Telos, a city built a mile or so beneath Mt. Shasta, California. During a recent trip to Mt Shasta, I encountered several local townspeople who had personally seen mysterious fires and lights on the slopes of Mt. Shasta, and have heard otherworldly chants and music late at night, emanating from the mountain. And of course, there have been sightings of mysterious robed people walking into the side of the mountain. Even the local visitor's guide mentions the Lemurian connection to Mt. Shasta!

This interview may really stretch your perception of reality. I hope it does. It's meant to. Sharula is Love and I am delighted to share her story with you.

INSIGHTS: Let's start off with some basic questions of who you are and where you are from.

SHARULA: My name is Sharula and I come from a city beneath Mt. Shasta, called Telos. The city was constructed about 14,000 years ago at the termination of the Lemurian continent. When the scientists and priests of Lemuria realized the continent was about to sink, they petitioned a group called the Agharta Network, which controlled all the subterranean cities, to build our own city beneath Mt Shasta.

There was an original set of caverns there. We chose to enlarge these caverns to make them bigger and more livable.

INSIGHTS: How large is Telos?

SHARULA: It's on five different levels. The bottom level is about 1 1/2 miles across, the other levels are different. The closest level to the mountain itself is only about three-quarters of a mile across.

INSIGHTS: How many people live in Telos?

SHARULA: A million and a half.

INSIGHTS: Tell us about your ecosystem; your water, food, air environment; what is it like to live in Telos?

SHARULA: We have perpetual light through a process of energizing stones to create full spectrum lighting. We process them with the forces that makes them small suns.

The five levels are garden levels where we produce all the food we need with hydroponic gardens. There are plants on all five levels that continue to circulate the air.

We work off the same system the earth does, the plants produce oxygen. Plus, we have air shafts that come through the surface that sends air. Since that air is polluted, we use them less and less.

INSIGHTS: What form of govemment do you have?

SHARULA: We have a system where the government is run by a council of twelve plus one. They are twelve masters, six male and six female. If anyone has a disagreement, they go to an arbitrator, rather than fight it out among themselves. All arbitrators report to the council and they change constantly. They are appointed to that position based on their natural affinity for it.

INSIGHTS: Who appoints them to thatposition?

SHARULA: The temple is run by the Melchezidek. Those in the temple, the high priests and high priestesses, are all ascended, therefore they are all working totally off God Consciousness, so that the human ego does not interfere at all with anything they do.

INSIGHTS: You mentioned that they are of Melchezidek?

SHARULA: All through the cosmos, there is an order called the Melchezidek. These are the beings who, through incarnation after incarnation, are the priests, the ones whove chosen to serve God, no matter what the guide might look like. They have donated their spiritual growth towards serving the Will of God. They are the cosmic priesthood you might say. There are several Melchezidek focuses on the planet at this time, one of them is the temple of Mt. Shasta.

INSIGHTS: You mean underneath Mt. Shasta?

SHARULA: Not only underneath is there the physical temple inside the city, but there is an ethereal temple that crowns Mt. Shasta. There's also a major Melchezidek retreat over Cuba which is run by one of the Archangels. And there's a Melchezidek retreat in Egypt.

INSIGHTS: And these are all in the etheric?

SHARULA: No, the one in Egypt is ethereal and in the physical also. There's one over South America and one in Moto Grosso, which is physical and that is where the Atlantean city is, in the Brazilian jungle.

INSIGHTS: Earlier, you mentioned that when your city was formed 14,000 years ago, you hade to petition the Agartha, the ones in charge of the inner earth cities. Are there other cities in existence?

SHARULA: Oh, yes. There are many. There are over one hundred inner earth cities. Some of them are very similar. The major one is called "Shamballa The Lesser." It's been in existence for a half million years. It was formed by a group of people called Hyprobeans or Trypoleans.

INSIGHTS: Where is Shamballa located?

SHARULA: It's at the center of the planet itself. In spite of what scientists have told people, it is not a raging ball of fire.

INSIGHTS: How does one travel from city to city or from surface to inner city?

SHARULA: Probably the most common

method is what we call the "tubes." It is a series of underground trains. We've bored tunnels that run underneath all the oceans and all the continents and connect all the cities and several of the retreats. The trains, which look very much like a subway train, are run on a cushion of air, an electromagnetic cushion, so they never actually touch the sides of the tunnel. This cushion creates a force field without friction and therefore they can achieve very high speeds. The trains are capable of running over 3,000 mph.

INSIGHTS: Between the surface and the inner cities, how does one travel?

SHARULA: There are several entrances that open to the surface. We'll use a ship which is run by the Silver Fleet.

INSIGHTS: The Silver Fleet.. explain that, please.

SHARULA: We are under the Ashtar Command and within this command are several fleets. The fleets native to Earth are the Silver Fleet. Earth is called a fallen planet, simply because it's fallen into the third dimension of consciousness and has remained there. The Silver Fleet is made up of beings from the Agarthean cities. Many of the ships that people see in the air are Silver Fleet ships, except for the "nasties."

INSIGHTS: How can one identify a Silver Fleet ship as opposed to the "hasties," as you call them?

SHARULA: All the Ashtar command ships, all the Confederation ships run from divine geometrics. The ships will be either cylinder or they will be saucer shaped or they will be round. There are not a lot of protrusions and angles; they have a tendency to be smooth. The ships that come in boomerang shapes and other weird configurations are usually not Confederation ships.

INSIGHTS: Let's talk about the people themselves, the Telosians. What would a typical Telosian look like?

SHARULA: The typical Telosian has a slightly golden tone to his skin and has a tendency toward high cheek bones and slightly almond-shaped eyes. Most Telosians run toward light hair and we have all eye colors. The men are generally 7‘ to 7'6" in height and the women are generally 6'6" to 7'1- in height. When we come to the surface we have a process of altering the molecules in our bodies so that we are able to appear the same height as people here on the surface.

INSIGHTS: Does your civilization have any of the social problems that ours seems to have, like population, hunger, homeless people and water droughts?

SHARULA: No. We don't have pollution because we are able to monitor our systems at all times. We have learned to accelerate the atom. When the first scientists started working with atoms they didn't realize that they weren't meant to shatter the atom for energy; they were meant to accelerate the atom for energy that won't die out and won't produce hazardous afterform. Because we learned to accelerate the atoms, we're also able to dematerialize all of our waste matter and return it back to its original form, which is the divine ethers in nonmaterial state.

INSIGHTS: Please share with us about how the women of Telos give birth to their children.

SHARULA: We have returned the process of childbirth to divine order. Women in third dimensional bodies were only meant to bear children in three months; it was not meant to be a nine month process. Even now a fetus is formed in three months. When a woman realizes that she is pregnant, she goes instantly into the temple and for 24 hours she is sealed in a chamber that produces absolutely nothing but beautiful images, beautiful sounds, beautiful thoughts and she is constantly told how beautiful she is and how perfect her child is. So, the very start of this life is impregnated in all the cells of their being with how perfect and how loved they are.

After three months, she returns to a birth chamber and a high priestess will put the mother in a slight altered state whereas she feels no pain, she's just happy and euphoric.

All the births take place underwater, which produces almost no labor pains. The mother feels nothing but pressure, she's not going through trauma. Because the mother is relaxed, the baby goes through less physical pain. When the baby is born in the water, both parents are there to hold it. They allow the baby to float underwater for some time until the baby itself chooses to come to the surface and breathe. And because there is no trauma about breathing, the baby has also learned to take complete breaths and they're not shut off immediately by panic and pain.

INSIGHTS: Is the U.S. Government aware of the existence of Telos and the other underground cities?

SHARULA: Yes. For a long time they have been trying to get in, to access the information of Telos and the Silver Fleet. The promise of what they need would be given to them, but in return there are several things they have to do or quit doing.

INSIGHTS: What was it that they were given to do or stop doing?

SHARULA: Basically, return the country to what it was founded on, and return to an open and honest government, so that every citizen has access to what's happening in the government.

INSIGHTS: Are you referring to the government's interaction with other extraterrestrials that are not of the Silver Fleet?

SHARULA: Yes, that is only one.

INSIGHTS: When was the government first introduced to Telos?

SHARULA: They have been aware of the subterranean cities and they have been aware of Telos since the country's conception. It is only near the turn of the century that they started taking action. This action did not get real aggressive until the 1950s.

INSIGHTS: In wrapping up, is there a special message thatyou'd like to share with our readers?

SHARULA: We have come up for a reason. We are not here for sightseeing. We have information that we are releasing to the people up here. Information on how to achieve the state of mastery, the state called ascension, how to return back to their God-Self We want to teach more and more people up here how to achieve freedom, where they are no longer tied to anything. Right now, I'm in the process of writing a book and I give workshops. My husband, Shield, and I are twin flames and we are achieving workshops around the country to help people to some of these processes. We're starting with the more simple knowledge which will lead to the more advanced. We are releasing the information that our people have been guarding for all these thousands of years.

It is the goal of the Hierarchy of this planet to unite the inner and the outer, as the inner cities and the outer cities become one. There are a few things that have to happen before that. We must achieve through our ambassadorships the exchange of information to awaken people to their potential, their Godhood, to their impending mastery. When the unification comes, the people in the outside cities will hold the same consciousness as the people in the inner cities.

Part Ten

Aliens & Atlanteans of Mount Shasta

By Commander X

According to the author of ***Underground Alien Bases and The Ultimate Deception***, there are at last count over 50 such bases being occupied by both "good" and "bad" ETs in the U.S. alone. One of the most active is to be found in Northern California.

One of the UFO underground bases the "good guys " are definitely in control of, is the base beneath Mt. Shasta in northern California.

The tunnels under Mt. Shasta are vast and house equipment and ships you wouldn't believe could possibly exist. There are teleportation and levitation devices, huge (by our definition) "Mother-Ships," and a crystal almost the size of a New York City skyscraper.

From all over the globe, hundreds of New Agers visit this site annually, and some even make this their home. Quite a number of "space channels," are known to operate in the area, such as Sister Thedra, who has been channeling Ashtar as well as other Space Guardians, not to mention Count Saint Germain, who has been known to visit here in his physical body from time to time.

Mt. Shasta is rich in the lore of the occult and metaphysics. It is truly a spiritual focal point for this planet. Deep from beneath the ground—where only the most aware are allowed—a full-time operation is constantly being carried out to save the Earth.

I have been told by sources whom I trust completely that the base was originally established by the people of Lemuria, a great continent that once existed in the middle of the Pacific; but just like its sister continent Atlantis, was destroyed due to the greedy nature and negativity of a few foolish leaders who were bent on planetary, as well as interplanetary, conquest.

So many "odd and peculiar" happenings have transpired around and in Mount Shasta that it would take several volumes to even penetrate the surface of all this material. The Lemurians, some of whom still reside here, are often seen wandering in the region. They can be recognized due to the fact that they are quite tall—in the eight and nine foot range. They even have their own underground city here, and it's all made of gold. Even the nature spirits—the gnomes, the elves and the fairies—run about here non-disturbed, and many "outsiders" will tell you that they've heard the sound of far away flutes, which are the favorite instrument of the elemental kingdom. The only "unusual dweller" around these parts I might be the least bit cautious of would be our hairy friend Bigfoot, who has been known to scare the living hell out of hikers who go away not being such "happy campers," mainly due to the somewhat nonappealing scent he has been known to toss off. I've been told that Mt. Shasta has a highly charged aura which prevents the forces of darkness from penetrating anywhere nearby. Teams of Lemurians, Space Brothers and elementals working jointly, meditate daily underground here to heal the planet and to keep this sacred spot safe from either physical or mental attack Those that have been in the tunnels underground are never the same, their whole life so changed by what they have seen and heard!

There is even one instance that I know of where a young woman—just recently married—was healed by the rays of a space ship that hovered over her small camp. Hanna Spitzer told her amazing story in an old issue of Tim Beckley's UFO Review, from which I have his permission to quote excerpts:

"My husband, Damian, and I came to Mt. Shasta just last September. We were drawn here by the majesty that surrounds this area. Damian had been here before and so he was familiar with the surrounding communities and the people who reside near this locale.

"Our closest friend, Patrick, a very talented young artist, had been my husband's companion on his earlier visit, and he also was captivated with Mt. Shasta. As luck had it, he was to be commissioned by a local restaurant owner to paint a huge mural of Mt. Shasta and the many legends that have long surrounded this magical mountain.

"Quickly, we moved up the side of the mountain and set up camp. From here we had a picturesque view of Mt. Shasta city. This tiny village consists of ski shops and sleepy little hide-a-ways, with a few occult bookstores and health food stores thrown in for good measures. At one of the stores, someone told us about a strange light that had been seen while this person was out camping on the same property where we were hving. Apparently, she awoke from a deep sleep and saw numerous flashing lights and heard a whooping noise.

"When she went into town the next morning she found that others had undergone similar experiences.

"Throughout our stay, Patrick kept telling us about a wonderful lady, a very gifted psychic, who was said to be a real 'powerhouse,' and who could attract a lot of phenomena herself. Her name was Aendreious, and Patrick had invited her to come and stay with all of us. I was really fascinated by what I had heard, and couldn't wait to meet this woman.

"One day when Damian was in town doing some chores a striking woman in a turban approached him. It was Aendreious. Damian brought her up to the land that afternoon and immediately we were struck by her presence. As gifts, she had brought each of us a crystal. She spoke in a very knowing manner. On top of this, she was very meditative and peaceful and extremely fascinated with the mountain. Through this lady we learned quite a lot about magnetism and attraction. I knew—as we all did—that if we were to have a sighting, it would be while she was living with us.

"Aendreious had a wonderful attitude about flying saucers and aliens. She thought of them as masters, not little green men to be aftaid. of. Her talking calmed me a bit and I soon lost any fear I might have had. For days the men had been teasing me about the dark and about creatures who would try to grab me and take me away.

"Going into town became an experience in itself. We loved to speak with the people there and hear about their experiences first hand. There was one charming lady who walked through the streets talking to everyone she met about the saucers. She always wore a shiny yellow hat and seemed very devoted to her task."

William E. Hamilton III—Bill to just about anyone who knows him—became fascinated with the mystery of Mt. Shasta after reading the book ***A Dweller on Two Planets***, by Phylos. This was even before his first visit to the mountain which—believe it or not—took place when he was just 15 years old.

I would suppose it was sometime later, however, that Bill actually began to look into the rumors and stories regarding underground bases which are known to crisscross this country—not to mention the rest of the worldl

Then finally in 1977, the veteran researcher whose work is highly respected by other UFOlogists, had a fimt-hand encounter with a young woman who sent his mind whirling and his thoughts buzzing. For this attractive, but very exotic looking lady revealed that she was not a full time inhabitant of our world, but was actually a resident of an underground city located at the very heart of Mt. Shasta. Extracts of what she revealed to Bill regarding her subterranean domain, and her people's origins, their ongoing contact with outer space beings, was all part of their conversation which took place during several meetings. The woman's story—as you will see in just a moment—is utterly fascinating and deserves the attention of anyone doing serious research into underground cities and bases.

The Girl From Beneath Mt. Shasta

I run across some fascinating people in the course of my investigations who tell me many unusual stories. While on the trail of reports of UFO base locations, I met a young, very pretty blonde girl with almond-shaped eyes and small perfect teeth, whose name was Bonnie. Bonnie has told me an incredible story and has related a volume of interesting information on Atlantis and Lemuria. Bonnie is sincere, cheerful, and rational, and says she is a Lemurian born under the sign of Leo in 1951 in a city called Telos that was built inside an artificial dome-shaped cavern in the Earth a mile or so beneath Mt. Shasta, California.

Bonnie, her mother, her father Ramu, her sister Judy, her cousins Lorae and Matox, live and move in our society, returning frequently to Telos for rest and recuperation.

Bonnie relates that her people use boring machines to bore tunnels in the Earth. These boring machines heat the rock to incandescence, then vitrify it, thus eliminating the need for beams and supports.

A tube transit train system is used to connect the few Atlantean/Lemurian cities that exist in various subterranean regions of our hemisphere. The tube trains are propelled by electromagnetic impulses up to speeds of 2500 mph. One tube connects with one of their cities in the Mato Grosse jungle of

Brazil. The Lemurians have developed space travel and some flying saucers come from their subterranean bases. Bonnie says her people are members of a federation of planets.

They grow food hydrophonically under full-spectrum lights with their gardens attended by automatons. The food and resources of Telos are distributed in plenty to the million-and-a-half population that thrives on a no-money economy. Bonnie talks about history, of the Uighers, Naga-Mayas, and Quetzels, of which she is a descendant. She recounts the destruction of Atlantis and Lemuria and of a war between the two superpowers fought with advanced weaponry. She says the Atlanteans built a huge crystal-powered beam weapon that was used to control a small moon of Earth with a missile to be aimed at China, but their plans went awry and the moon split in two, coming down into the Atlantic, north of Bermuda, deluging the remaining isle of Atlantis. She claims her people are now part of a much greater underground kingdom called Agharta, ruled by a super race she calls "Hyprobeans."

I met Bonnie's cousin, Matox, who, like her, is a strict vegetarian and holds the same attitudes concerning the motives of government. They constantly guard against discovery or intrusion. Their advanced awareness and technology helps them to remain vigilant. Will we openly meet these long-lost relatives of ours? Bonnie says yes, but this is part of her incredible mission. Her mission: to warn those who will listen of the coming cataclysms that will culminate at the end of the century in a shift of the Earth's axis. After this catastrophe, she says the world will be one, and the survivors will build a new world free of worry, poverty, disease and exploitation. The world will exist on a higher plane of vibrations and man will come to know his true history and heritage.

Science fiction? Bonnie is a real person. Many have met her. Is she perpetrating a hoax? For what motive? She does not seek publicity and I had a devil of a time getting her to meetings to talk with others, but she has done so. There has been little variation in her story or her answers in the past three years. She has given me excellent technical insight on the construction of a crystal powered generator that extracts ambient energy. She has given me new insights on UFOs and their purpose in coming here. Bonnie's father, the Ramu, is 300 years old and a member of the ruling council of Telos.

Many tunnels are unsafe and closed off. All tube transit tunnels are protected and are designed to eject uninvited guests. Does Bonnie have the answers that we are looking for? I don't know. I am not making the claims nor can I provide proof. Bonnie says she would like to satisfy our need for proof and will work with me on a satisfactory answer to that problem, but she is unconcerned with whether people accept her or not. Bonnie is humorous and easygoing and well-poised, yet sometimes she becomes brooding and mysterious. She says her people are busy planning survival centers for refugees. One of these is to be near Prescott, Arizona.

Following is a question and answer session between Mr. Hamilton and Bonnie, which was done to answer even more questions about this underground world we are so intrigued by:

Q. Were there ten races on Lernuria?

A. They were called sub-races. There was only one race.

Q: Can you date that?

A. That was approximately 200,000 years ago.

Q. You once said that the early Lernurians come from the planetAurora?

A. Yes, and at that time the sun (of Earth) was giving off entirely too much radiation, resulting in shorter life spans. The Hyprobeans went inside this planet. They entered at the polar entrances, inside of which there is another sun which has no radioactive effect. These people still live there in the major city of Shamballa. They are still ruled by the hereditary King of the World. The people who remained on top degenerated into what we call the Fourth Race.

Q. Did they continue to degenerate?

A. They continued to degenerate. There came to be more differences in the races.

They started mental degeneration on the point of warring on each other.

when the Earth was forming, huge gas pockets were formed, cavities within the Earth, some of which were just a few feet wide, but thousands of miles long. The scientists started detecting the weakening of the Archean gas chambers on their instruments. This was about 15,000 years ago and at that time the Earth's magnetic field was getting very erratic.

Q. Did you have contact with extraterrestrials at that time?

A. At that time we were still in contact with the Federation. Lemuna and Atlantis were both members of the Federation.

Q. Did they have air travel and space travel?

'A. Yes, they did. Atlantis and Lemuria could both travel to other planets.

Q. What was it that destroyed Atlantis?

A. After the destruction of Lemuria, which was caused by natural catastrophe, for a long time the planet was unstable, for about 200 or 300 years. The pyramids were built before the destruction of Lemuria. At this time the Atlanteans were becoming difficult and several of them who believed in the Law of the One did not care for what the scientists were doing. The scientists were experimenting with monster crystals that had unbelievable power.

Q. were there any biological experiments like cloning or with DNA?

A. Yes, there were. This had been going on for hundreds of years by that time. They were using the "things" as their slaves. Some people left Atlantis at this time and came to Mt. Shasta where the Lemurians had built a city called Telos.

Q. Now the Atlanteans started experimenting with huge crystals—were these the fire crystals?

A. Yes, they generated cosmic energy. It is the cut of the crystal which causes the generation (wavelength?). It draws out of the atmosphere (the energy) and generates it into a high force and higher vibration. It has no moving parts. The crystal has an inner fire—they change colors. The crystals the Atlanteans used built up energy they could not control.

Q. Is this the secret of the power source on flying saucers?

A. Yes, a lot of it is crystals, particularly the atmospheric vehicles. The planet-to-planet vehicles are driven by an Ion-mercury engine. Spaceships can reach speeds way beyond light—they can enter hyperspace you generate into the fourth dimension. This is controlled by an onboard computer that takes you into and out of hyperspace. I know this is a simplification. When you're on a ship going into hyperspace, you will hear this vibration and a loud screaming sound when you enter, then you will hear nothing. (I have had many correlations on this data and am researching it further toward a comprehensive theory of space travel).

Q. Do you travel between galaxies?

A. Yes, that is usually when you enter hyperspace when you are going a far, far distance.

Q. Have you heard stories of any advanced beings out there?

A. Yes, they are near the center of the Universe.

Q. What is at the Center?

A. We call it the seat of God—the generation of energy.

William Hamilton should be congratulated on his being such an energetic and dedicated seeker of truth in this field. He has spent tireless hours without thought of remuneration and has personally neglected any fanfare in order to pierce through the fog of misinformation that is so often placed in our path. Those interested in finding out more about Bill's work can write the publisher for information on his privately published manuscript ***Alien Magic,*** and his group, ***UFORCES.***

Certainly, he is one of those who can testify that the truth will set us all free!

Travel To The Center Of The Earth
And Find It Teeming With Life!

By Timothy Green Beckley

You can bet your Slim Jim that the Earth is a stranger place than you ever thought it could be.

Frankly, the text books – the truth according to our "experts" – are all wrong!

If you think life exists only on the surface of the planet you have been listening to the "party line" way too long, for there are those who see the Earth as being multilayered, and that what goes on "above" definitely goes on "below."

I remember back in the 1960s reading an ad that ran in just about every pulp magazine about a book by Dr. Raymond

Bernard on how flying saucers were NOT from outer space but came from inside the earth. It constituted a preposterous statement if there ever was one – or at least so I thought in my early teens.

Truth is, the first book I wrote (and if you include the efforts of other authors whom we have published, that figure is now over two hundred UFO and paranormal titles) and had published by Gray Barker's Saucerian Press was a mighty tome that still remains in print in one form or another. **The Shaver Mystery and the Inner Earth** went into several printings and eventually evolved into **Subterranean World Inside Earth,** which has sold year after year, decade after decade, and has even been translated into Japanese and Korean.

Of course, stories about traveling to various locales inside the Earth are nothing new.

Hell, isn't Hell located inside the Earth somewhere in a fiery pit?

Everyone must have read Jules Verne's **Journey To The Center Of The Earth**, so frankly there isn't anything new under the sun – even the central sun said to light the interior of our planet.

This book is a gem – of that I am certain!

The story of the **Smoky God** is dramatic and tells of a fantastic journey by father and son to a place inhabited by gentle giants. And we have even included the article by Ray Palmer that broke the ice so to speak, offering evidence in an early issue of **Flying Saucers From Other Worlds** magazine that there are entrances to the Hollow Earth at the North and South Pole. And, by damn, where else are you going to find an interview with the fabulous "Princess Sharula" from the imposing underground city of Telos?

We've updated and expanded this edition to include a great deal of pertinent information on this controversial Hollow Earth theory.

The venerable Brad Steiger leads us on an expedition to ancient Atlantis and offers an Inner Earth tie-in, while paranormal researcher Scott Corrales dabbles in the murky world of UFOs and Ultra-Terrestrials, offering substantiation that, indeed, something weird is, pardon the expression, underfoot, and that flying saucers and their strange occupants do not have to come from beyond the stars but may have their origins closer than most of us care to imagine.

And then there is Sean Casteel, who leads us through the cavern-bound existence of the late Richard Shaver. Shaver stimulated interest in the Inner Earth for several decades after offering up his "I Remember Lemuria" manuscript that appeared in the March, 1945 edition of **Amazing Stories**, a pulp science fiction magazine who confronted its readers with the unnerving realization that Shaver's contributions were more FACT than fiction!

So it's all here for you to ponder and enjoy.

The cards are on the table and the last vessel to the underworld is about to leave dry dock. Join us on a voyage like you've never taken before – a voyage to THE CENTER OF THE EARTH!

THE COSMIC BATTLE HAS BEGUN!

Inner Earth People vs. Outer Space Aliens

The Teachings Of Rev. William L. Blessing

Tim Beckley, editor of the Conspiracy Journal and prominent UFO publisher, notes: "Back when I was just beginning my research into esoteric matters, I was bombarded with Christian-oriented literature, much of which was pseudo-religious with a decidedly right-wing spin; some of it even peppered with Nazi and KKK propaganda. Little of it addressed concerns of UFOs or metaphysics. If anything, it usually slammed such matters, directly implicating Mr. Scratch (aka Satan) as being behind such phenomenon.

"One newsletter did catch my attention, however. It was edited by Rev. William L. Blessing, who was courageous enough to delve into the mysteries of the universe, tackling inner earth and UFO mysteries as hardly any other cleric would dare.

"From time to time, Rev. Blessing would compile his various sermons into large philosophical discourses. One large size volume that was published around 1965 was a controversial tome that apparently was taken out of circulation. Inner Earth People / Outer Space Beings is a huge collection of Rev. Blessings teachings which were nearly lost to time, had I not come across this 320+ page massive undertaking in a rare book collection.

"Because of the conflict in the world today and the increase in UFO sightings, I personally feel that this work should reach as wide an audience as possible."

* * * * *

Rev. Blessing stated:

The Bible teaches us that there are beings dwelling inside the earth. For want of a better term, I shall call them the Inner Earth People. I estimate the population of Inner Earth to be ten billion. There are

200,000,000 pilots in the flying saucer corps. They will quite soon invade the surface of the planet and, indeed, that invasion may have already begun by an advanced recon force that is flying out over the surface of earth, mapping land areas and strategic places where they will launch their primary strikes during the all-out invasion.

"And the four angels were loosed, which were prepared for an hour, and a day, and a month, and a year, to slay the third part of men. And the number of the army and horsemen were two hundred thousand thousand; and I heard the number of them." (Rev. 9:15-16)

That is two hundred million aviators of flying saucers. They look exactly like surface dwelling humans and their flying saucers are made of a type of metal that is plated with gold. "The sound of their wings was as of the sound of chariots." (Rev. 9:9)

"And the fifth angel sounded, and I saw a star fall from heaven unto the earth; and to him was given the key to the bottomless pit. And he opened the bottomless pit; and there arose a smoke out of the pit as the smoke of the great furnace; and the sun and the air were darkened by reason of the smoke of the pit. And there came out of the smoke locusts upon the earth; and unto them were given power as the scorpions of the earth have power." (Rev. 9:1-3) They are bringing a cloud of darkness, a mist, a smog, a cloud over the cities that they are mapping out, such as Los Angeles, London and elsewhere. But when the all-out invasion begins they will blanket the whole earth in darkness. "It shall be one day which shall be known to the Lord; neither night nor day." (Zech. 14:7).

Their vehicles were well known to the ancient prophets and was best described by Ezekiel: "And I looked and behold, a whirlwind came out of the north, a great cloud, and a fire enfolding itself, and a brightness was about it, and out of the midst thereof as the color of amber, out of the midst of the fire. Also out of the midst thereof came the likeness of four living creatures. And this was their appearance: they had the likeness of a man. And every one had four faces, and every one had four wings. And their feet were straight feet, and the sole of their feet was like the sole of a calf's foot; and they sparkled like the color of burnished brass. And they had the hands of man under their wings on their four sides; and they four had their faces and their wings. The wings were joined one to another; they turned not when they went; they went every one straight forward. As for the likeness of their faces, they four had the face of a man, and the face of a lion on the right side; and they four had the face of an ox on the left side; they four also had the face of an eagle. Thus were their faces; and their wings were stretched upward; two wings of every one were joined one to another; and two covered their bodies. And they went every one straight forward: whither the spirit was to go, they went; and they turned not when they went. As for the likeness of living creatures, their appearance was like burning coals of fire, and the appearance of lamps: it went up and down among the living creatures; and the fire was bright, and out of the fire went forth lightning. And the living creatures ran and returned as the appearance of a flash of lightning. (Ezek)

They will constantly beam messages to us. They will fly on magnetic lines, advancing from one point to another almost instantly, reversing their course or position more rapidly than the human eye can follow, using the power of levitation—reverse gravitation.

The inner earth people are of several different races and orders. Some originally lived on the surface, but some of them once lived above the earth in outer space. Long ago, they invaded the earth from space. The book of Genesis describes them as the "serpent" people.

"And it came to pass, when men began to multiply in the earth, and daughters were born to them, that the sons of God saw that the daughters of men that they were fair; and they took them wives of all which they chose. And the Lord said, My spirit shall not always strive with man, for that he also is flesh: yet his days shall be a hundred and twenty years. There were giants in the earth in those days; and also after that when the sons of God came in unto the daughters of men, and they bare children to them, the same became mighty men which were of old, men of renown. The earth also was corrupted before God; and the earth was filled with violence. And God looked upon the earth, and, behold, it was corrupt for all flesh had corrupted His way upon the earth." (Gen. 6:4; 11-12).

The invaders from space came originally from twenty-two different dwelling places in outer space and the names of the leaders of each of the outer space places that led a host of their people to the earth are as follows:

1. Samyaza,
2. Urakabarameel,
3. Akibeel,
4. Tamiel,
5. Ramuel,
6. Danel,
7. Azkeel,
8. Sarakuyal,
9. Asael,

10. Armers,

11. Batrael,

12. Anane,

13. Zavebe,

14. Samsaveel,

15. Etrael,

16. Turel,

17. Yomyael,

18. Arazyal,

19. Atnzarak,

20. Barkayal,

21. Barkayal Tamiel,

22. Asaradel.

(Book of Enoch, Ch 7 & 8)

Just exactly how many followers each leader brought with him to earth is not known but, at any rate, they materialized their bodies just like earth people and remained in the flesh and married women of earth. The children of these invaders were called "giants," many of them malformed, having six fingers and six toes. (1 Chron. 20:6) We do not say that all the offspring were malformed but many of them were. There was undoubtedly a race of giants ten to twelve feet tall and also a race of pygmies produced by the crossing of these outer space people with the women on the earth. The first generation of these people were not sterile, but there is evidence that the second generation were sterile hybrids who could not reproduce.

This crossing over and mixing of the outer space invaders with the women on the earth continued for 1,656 years; that is, from the time that Adam left the garden of Eden until the final days of Noah. (Gen. 5:1-32) All the inhabitants of the earth had become sterile one hundred years before the flood. The last children born on earth before the flood were the triplet sons of Noah: Shem, Ham and Japheth. They were born on Noah's 500th birthday. (Gen. 5:32) From that time until the flood, no children were born on earth. Consequently, no person on earth was drowned in the flood until one hundred years of age, for no children had been born for one hundred years.

Incidentally, in passing, it must be stated that the degeneracy of the earth before the flood was indescribable. Not only had the outer space people crossed with women, but men had corrupted themselves with animals as well, "for all flesh had corrupted his way upon the earth." (Gen. 6:12) Many of the animals we are forbidden to eat are part human. I could go into detail about this, describing the human marks in the bodies of each of the unclean animals, but suffice it to say that the serpent has a pelvic bone, as well as the remnants of arms and legs and gives birth to its young. It is too long a story to point out the human marks in each of the unclean animals, but they all have them. The hog does not chew cud and has a stomach like a human.

The space people who invaded earth—fallen angels, if you wish to call them that—together with their hybrid offspring who were giants and pygmies, were all sent into the inner earth just before the flood. Later, and various intervals since the flood, some of the earth people have been banished to the inner earth. "And the earth opened her mouth, and swallowed them up, and their houses, and all the men that appertained to Korah, and all their goods. They, and all that appertained to them, went down alive into the pit and the earth closed upon them; and they perished from among the congregation." (Num. 16: 32-33)

* * * * * *

DEEP UNDERGROUND:

In Search Of Dark Realms

By Scott Corrales

Having written on two previous occasions on the subject of subterranean societies, it is remarkable that more information continues to emerge on strange activities taking place here and now and involving an inordinate interest in the bowels of our world, not for the traditional activities of mining and oil drilling, but an active searching for something that may prove of interest to those living aboveground. Are the world's surface powers actively searching for a subterranean society that may have existed for millennia undetected by us? Is there any connection to the alleged underground "UFO bases" that filled newspaper and magazine headlines in the 1990's? Are we witnessing a new crop of "Aghartha searchers" in the tradition of the ones who went looking for this improbable realm in the early decades of the 20th century?

Trapped Underground?

The news item could not have been timelier. In March 2004, a team of six British explorers—archaeologists by some accounts, prospectors and military men in others —was trapped in the stygian gloom of the twenty mile-long Al Pazat cavern system in the Mexican village of Cuezatlán (state of Puebla). The explorers had been surprised by the sudden flooding of one of the cavern chambers and had managed to survive by climbing onto a giant underground boulder that literally kept them high and dry. Communicating with the surface world through a satellite phone, the six men called for help and the British embassy in Mexico City arranged to have a team of Royal Navy divers dispatched to the cave to find the stranded explorers. There would be nothing straightforward about this rescue effort – the divers would have to plunge into icy cold water, swim to a depth of one hundred meters (200 ft. approximately) to emerge into what speleologists were referring to as an air bubble. The rescue effort would also involve bringing the six men back through the frigid depths to the surface.

In spite of these dramatic details, the most curious fact remained that no one was quite sure about the identity of the party trapped underground. The British embassy characterized them as "speleologists" while the BBC described them as "soldiers". Villagers who had spoken to them before they ventured underground had described them as "veterans of the Gulf War". Journalists settled on the notion that they were uranium prospectors who had employed satellite imagery to identify the cavern system as a suitable location for finding fissionable materials.

Jesus Gonzalez Galicia, mayor of Cuezatlan, noted that the small size of his village allowed people to take a good look at their visitors from overseas. The group had entered into a bar for drinks and locals soon learned that their number included spelunkers, engineers and several Gulf War veterans, although the mixed group had never made the reason for its visit to the caves very clear.

Subsequently, British intelligence officials would confirm that the team's objectives were clearly military, prompting the Mexican press to describe the operation as "a foreign military incursion" in Mexican territory, something not seen since the early 20th century. Even concerned messages crossed the Atlantic between the Mexican state department and the British Foreign Office, more villagers stated that these visits had been going on for more than a decade, involving not only British personnel but Americans as well.

Upon learning of the military identity of the persons trapped in the Cuetzalán cave system, Puebla governor Melquiades Morales observed that they had already committed a serious violation by conducting any type of activity other than sightseeing, which is what a tourist visa allows. When rescued, the parties involved would be deported and declared personae non grata.

Experts argued as to what the "real" reasons for the British military team's visit could be. Many insisted on the highly rational answer offered by the search for uranium and other radioactive materials, even as Jose Antonio Montaño, president of the Union Mexicana de Agrupaciones Espeleológicas (Mexican Speleological Association), insisted that fissionables couldn't possibly be found in Cuetzalán, since the cave system's interior is completely made of calcium carbonate, formed over the hundreds of millions of years by unicellular organisms and coral.

What then were these specialists doing in the depths of Mexico? Speculation has run the gamut from a search for hidden alien bases to lost Aztec treasure that escaped the rapacity of the Conquistadors, but an increasing number of researchers believe that the marooned British expedition – whose rescue was accomplished a week later amid international controversy – was looking for the legendary tunnel or tunnels linking the Americas and built by an antediluvian civilization.

The Tunnels Of Light

Controversy has raged since the 1970's regarding the infamous Ecuadorian tunnels described by Erich Von Daniken in "The Gold of the Gods" —supposedly lined with sheets of gold that recounted the hidden history of the human race – and more levelheaded reports on such artificial structures presented in specialized journals such as *Pursuit*. We needn't go as far south as Ecuador to find a belief in similar underground structures. Mexico allegedly boasts as intricate a network of artificial tunnels as anyone could wish, running from the American Southwest down into Central America, and crafted by an unknown civilization whose recollection has survived purely in the form of oral traditions.

One such tradition can be found in the lands surrounding the urban sprawl of Mexico City and has to do with the unearthly landscape of the Teotihuacán pyramid complex northeast of the city. This "City of the Gods" that was old when the first Aztec wanderers entered the region known as Anáhuac supposedly contains an entrance to a city that can be reached through a series of tunnels – a city known only as the "dwelling place of the white god". While caves have indeed been found under the massive Pyramid of the Sun, and which are believed to have housed a form of worship different from that held above (a more matriarchal, Earth-goddess worship opposed to the Sun-god reverenced at the pyramid's summit) no traces of these means of access have been found. However, in the western state of Jalisco preserves a similar belief – underground tunnels can lead the seeker to the temple of the "Emperor of the World".

The indefatigable Andreas Faber Kaiser wrote about a tribe of light-skinned Indians dwelling on the border between Mexico and Guatemala who spoke openly of the belief in an "extensive tunnel network" under the area occupied by the Lacandon tribe. This belief, which dovetails interestingly enough with that of the Tayu

Wari tunnels of Ecuador, claims that golden tablets can be found which tell the story of the human race...but as with all such stories, the locals are vague about the details. All that is known for sure is that in 1689 a Spanish monk, Francisco Antonio Fuentes, wrote in glowing terms about a magnificent artificial structure, "the marvelous tunnels of Puchuta" in what is now Guatemala, which run underground from the aforementioned town to the community of Tecpan, some twenty-five miles away. Was this a spur or connection to the "main network" of tunnels linking the continent? Other traditions described Indian raiders making use of the tunnels to harass the early Spanish settlers, since contrary to what one might believe, the underworld was "filled with light" of some sort. One of these subterranean arteries, accessible from an unspecified building in Santa Cruz del Quiché, would allow a traveler to enter Mexico in about an hour – a journey of at least two days using the twisting and turning mountain paths of the surface world.

Belief in underground cities remains a fundamental tenet of contemporary contactee beliefs, as exemplified by an April 2004 news item discussing the theories posited by Argentinean ufologist-turned-contactee Pedro Romaniuk, 82, a former airline pilot who authored over twenty books on UFOs and went on to become one of his country's best-known contactees.

Romaniuk firmly believes that under the bedrock of the Andean Range and especially near the city of Cachi, there lies an inner earth empire populated by beings of Atlantean descent, and in which can be found all manner of animals ranging from exotic prehistoric survivals to mutants produced by the arcane science of the inner-earthers.

Nor are his theories restricted exclusively to planet Earth: NASA, believes Romaniuk, will never find life on Mars despite its best efforts and keen scientific know-how, because the Red Planet "is hollow and contains a great civilization in possession of ten million interstellar spacecraft ready for takeoff," – a notion that conjures up images of harried Martian space traffic controllers trying to clear these vehicles for launch at the same time.

"The Andean cordillera," Romaniuk told reporters from Salta's El Tribuno newspaper, "is hollow. And it is specifically here that one can find an intraterrestrial realm inhabited and controlled by the descendants of ancient Atlantis, who are in possession of a superior technology. Many of the creatures that people claim having seen, such as the improperly termed Chupacabras, are the result of the genetic experimentation of the subterranean scientists. Romaniuk tentatively extended this explanation to account for the bizarre hairy hominid of Rosario de la Frontera, although he also allowed for the possibility that "an act of natural serendipity" could have created the Argentinean Bigfoot.

Almost a year earlier, Romaniuk had commissioned two scientists from his "Fundación Instituto Biofísico de Investigaciones" (FICI) to conduct a survey that would prove the existence of the underground post-Atlantean civilization to a disbelieving world. In May 2003, Omar

Hesse and Jorge Millstein conducted a survey of the general region surrounding the city of Cachi. After concluding operations, they announced that uncommon radioactive signatures and microwaves had been detected from a source beneath the Earth's surface.

Somewhere under the massive peak known as Nevado de Cachi, the scientists concluded, was something that generated alternating electrical waves—possibly the advanced machinery of Romaniuk's putative intraterrestrials. "The oscillations clearly indicate that there is activity kilometers beneath the surface," Omar Hesse told the El Tribuno newspaper, "which means a power source. This could mean engines."

His partner Jorge Millstein cautioned that it would be necessary to return to this area with something he termed "depth rods" in order to ascertain more precise readings, reminding journalists that the area tested happened to be "one of the hottest" as regarded UFO activity, mentioning a strip of anomalous occurrences between the towns of La Poma and Cayafate.

A report provided by Argentina's Grupo CATENT and entitled "El Rosario, The Subterranean City of La Rioja") states that on September 23, 1970, a shepherd from the Pre-Cordilleran region near Cerro del Rosario sought to shelter his sheep from torrential rains in a nearby cave. As he ventured deeper into its recesses while the downpour continued outside, the shepherd claimed to have found a "flight of steps" leading downward and counted three hundred sixty of them as they led him deeper into the bowels of the earth. Upon reaching the bottom of the steps, he was stunned to find himself in an underground city filled with eldritch metallic buildings capped with domes, transparent sidewalks and strange, silent vehicles that hovered only a few feet off the surface. He suddenly found himself being stared at by strange humanlike beings standing in excess of seven feet in height, some wearing black tunics and others white ones.

Like the protagonist of "Etidorpha", the shepherd walked trance-like along a given street, taking in the odd landscape, until he came to another staircase identical to the one that led him downward. He ascended the steps and found himself in the surface world (no mention is made of whether the shepherd was able to find his flock again in the original cave). Excited, he ventured down to a nearby town and contacted a local priest and a physician, who listened to his account. When officials of the government of La Rioja visited the site, all they could find was "an unbreachable stone wall" at the end of the cave....

While these cases, despite their intriguing nature, have an undeniable element of fancy attached to them, there are documented discoveries of tunnels in the Andes, notably in Perú. Spain's EFE news agency ran a story on March 9, 2003 announcing the discovery of a series of underground vestibules, rooms, waterworks and ancient tombs under the city of Cuzco, the capital of the Inca Empire.

A Spanish archaeologist, Anselmo Pi, as part of the Wiracocha Project that kicked off in August 2000, discovered the 2 kilometer-long tunnel joining the enigmatic, cyclopean-walled Sacsahuamán fortress outside of Cuzco with the Koricancha temple in the city.

In a presentation to the Cultural Commission of Peru's legislative assembly, Anselmo Pi noted that the discovery of the tunnel "may change perspectives on Peruvian history."

The radar imaging obtained by the Wirakocha Project suggests that the tunnel links directly not only to the Koricancha or "Temple of the Sun", but to other structures as well, including such temple structures as the Colcampata and the Huamanmarca.

Although knowledge of a tunnel entrance at the Sacsahuamán Fortress is widespread, this gateway to the tunnel system was shut down in the 1920s after a number of curiosity-seekers vanished in its labyrinthine depths. The culture responsible for the tunnel's construction, said Pi, would involve a pre-Inca civilization "that has yet to be considered....the great question is ascertaining what age [the tunnel] belonged to."

The Wirakocha Project's efforts at confirming and mapping the legendary underground galleries would help to substantiate the accounts of Spanish chroniclers like Pedro Cieza de León, who wrote of the existence of a citadel under Cuzco.

Down Other Tunnels....

There is something about the Balearic Islands that makes them appealing – not just to the beach and nightclub crowd that has made Ibiza, Mallorca and Minorca some of the hottest entertainment spots in Europe – but to conquerors throughout history: Carthaginians, Romans, Byzantines, Arabs, British and French, who riddled the island with fortifications in their respective time periods. In the 18th century, when the island of Minorca was in the hands of the British Empire, a series of tunnels were built to provide communications with different outposts, including a fabled "underwater tunnel" that allegedly connected with forts on the other islands, and which archaeologists have never found.

These military tunnels were not new constructions: they were merely expansions and refurbishments of older tunnels hewn by unknown hands, possibly the authors of similar underground passages on the island of Malta. The Minorcan tunnel system was built on three levels and contains passageways that branch out in every direction; some of the tunnels have been described as "enormous" and have vaulted ceilings some 20 feet tall. Researchers who have ventured into the underground warren of forgotten tunnels have likened them to the ancient city of Derinkuyu in the Cappadocian region of Turkey.

In an article for Spain's Enigmas magazine, Minorca native Natacha Méndez, states that aside from the tunnels it is also possible to find caves near the coast that have man-made staircases leading to deep passageways whose ultimate purpose has never been ascertained. The capital city of Mahón is reputedly built on hundreds of such passages that form "impossible labyrinths", in Méndez's words, and which have never been properly documented by academe. The sea has invaded many of these passageways, making them inaccessible, as is the case with the Taula de Torralba pit, which descends over one hundred twenty feet into the earth.

Méndez's article speculates that the tunnels under "Fort Marlborough" on Minorca were destroyed by the retreating British army to keep them from the advancing French, but wonders if denial of use was in fact the real reason f their destruction. Had the invaders made a discovery that they wished to keep from others? The author believes that the tunnels of Minorca may lead to a central location, suggesting that like Derinkuyu, the island of Minorca was inhabited by unknown beings in the distant past.

In March 2003, Argentina's prestigious Clarín newspaper published an intriguing magazine article regarding the claims of a Japanese newsman Shun Akiba, whose credentials include being the only foreign journalist to cover the Gulf War directly from Baghdad (aside from CNN's Peter Arnett), claimed that an enigmatic underground city existed under the megalopolitan spread of modern Tokyo. His research into the subject was condensed into a single volume – *Tokyo, Imperial City: The Secret of a Hidden Underground Network* – which promptly sold out several editions.

A trip to a second-hand bookstore, writes Akiba, led him to find an old map of the Japanese capital – a map that showed substantial differences when compared with a current city plan. In the vicinity of the Parliament building, for example, the author noticed that two subway lines were shown as running parallel to each other in the old map, while the newer map showed them as intersecting. The variations appeared in other subway stops as well, particularly those adjacent to the Prime Minister's home. A thorough search of construction records was fruitless and the public works departments proved particularly unhelpful. Akiba had no choice but to do the legwork, or rather, the rail-work: he boarded the subway "once, twice, thousands of times" and looked at places that most straphangers tend to ignore on their way to work or back home.

Akiba reached the conclusion that the tunnels not shown on the official maps of the Tokyo underground aren't one or two, but many. According to the government, the Japanese capital has a dozen subway lines for a total of two hundred fifty kilometers of tunnels; the author of the controversial book contradicts this official figure, stating that the tunnels surpass the two thousand kilometer mark. He concludes that the underground complexes "fenced in" by the rerouted train lines must have been built during the tensions of a possible global thermonuclear war between 1950 and the late 1980s. The Tokyo city government has dismissed Akiba's findings as wild speculation, politely suggesting that Akiba "became paranoid after working in so many war zones."

Conclusion

This work has presented three clearly defined types of underground structure: some of the tunnels described are objectively real; others are enshrouded in legend, while still others belong to the realm of the metaphysical. There is an undeniable protean quality at work here that morphs legend into reality and into other levels of understanding, possibly connected to the human attraction and revulsion of the dark spaces that exist under our feet.

UNDERGROUND EMPIRES:
Fact Or Fiction?

Subterranean cities and temples played a major role in pre-European Latin American societies: religious rites of all kinds were held in these underground locations and tradition holds they were used as aumbries for the storage of treasure and forgotten lore. Still other traditions hold that these underground facilities were not built by the civilizations to which historians and archaeologists usually ascribe their provenance, but by ancient "elder races" whose only remains can be found in mysterious megalithic constructions around the world.

Official science pays no mind to this speculation, dismissing it with the same certainty as they would brush aside the factuality of the video game "Tomb Raider" (which follows the exploits of cyberheroine Lara Croft through a number of underground Andean locations). But can we really be so sure?

The Quest For Lost Chincana

Dr. Raul Rios Centeno of Peru's INDECOPI organization formed part of a six-man team (five researchers and a guide) who braved the dizzying altitude of Andes to go in search of La Chincana, the subterranean city located beneath the former Inca capital of Cuzco.

On July 15, 1998, after undergoing a brief acclimatization period to the 3500 meter elevation of Cuzco, Dr. Rios's team met up with Inez Puente de la Vega, a historian whose knowledge of Inca culture and command of the Runa-Simi variant of the Quechua language would prove of great help in their expedition.

The group's initial efforts focused on finding a point of access to the fabled Chincana: locals informed them that one of the main entrances to the underground city was precisely beneath the Sacsahuayman archaeological fortress — whose giant stonework is pre-Inca in origin — about a kilometer away from Cuzco. Other sources hinted at the existence of two other gateways: one in the Koricancha or Palace of the Sun, which was partially demolished during the Colonial period to build the Carmelite Monastery, and still another beneath Cuzco's great cathedral.

Not surprisingly, scholars at the University of San Antonio de Abad and the Andean University, both of them in Cuzco, refused to speak to the explorers about the putative underground city. But as chance would have it, the Rios party managed to gain access to the Andean University's library, where a fascinating piece of information was uncovered.

In 1952, a group of twelve explorers—a mixed group of French and American researchers—managed to gain access through the Sacsahuayman entrance with enough provisions to last for five days as they embarked upon what they termed "the greatest discovery since Machu

Picchu".

The team ventured into the Sacsahuayman entrance and nothing further was heard from them until fifteen days later, when French explorer Phillipe Lamontierre emerged from the hole suffering from acute dementia and with visible signs of malnourishment and even the bubonic plague (attributable, says Dr. Rios, to the bats inhabiting the underground spaces). The broken survivor indicated that his fellow adventurers had died, and some of them had even fallen down unfathomed abysses. Among his belongings was an ear of corn made of solid gold, which was later entrusted to the Cuzco Museum of Archeaology (no indication is given as to whether it is on display or not).

While sobered by the Lamontierre experience, Dr. Rios' group resolutely asked the National Institute of Culture's authorization to enter the depths at their own risk, and requesting that the concrete plug covering the entrance be demolished.

Officialdom turned a deaf ear to this plea, and the group had to find more devious ways of accomplishing its objectives.

Having given "valuable consideration" to the security guards at Sacsahuayman, the Rios group managed to get into one of the connecting chambers to the underground complex. Equipped with infrared goggles, the group penetrated a chamber that measured scarcely 1.13 meters from the door's stone frame to the rocky floor. "The stench within the [connecting chamber]," writes Dr. Rios, "was nauseating, as it had been employed as a latrine for sometime. For some strange reason, the stonework did not reflect infrared rays. However, with the aid of our friend Jorge Zegarra, we were able to apply a RAD-2 X-ray filter, which provided a radio-opacity of 400 to 600% that of aluminum."

"It was thus that we reached a hallway whose height progressively diminished until reaching a scant 94 centimeters," continues his letter. "and given that our average height is 1.80 meters, we had no choice but to return to our starting point."

The Rios party tried to obtain readings on their Geiger counter without much success, but through the RAD-2 X-ray filter, they managed to secure a number of photos which led them to the conclusion that "a coating of some dense metal"—comparable to lead—existed within the hallways, and that there were cracks in the stonework which indeed allowed for the passage of X-rays.

At this point, the guide abandoned the mission out of a very real fear of reprisals by the Culture Institute.

Dr. Rios concludes his letter by saying that the images captured by means of the RAD-2 device were being analyzed by Carlos Garcia and Guillermo LaRosa Richardson of the School of Engineering in Lima, Peru.

The Amazing Story Of Juan Moricz

The name of Juan Moricz—a Hungarian

nobleman turned Argentinean citizen—stands heads and shoulders above all others in these accounts of subterranean lairs in South America.

Indefatigable author and investigator Magdalena del Amo-Freixedo met Moricz in Ecuador and was able to hear from the late miner/explorer's very lips the story of how he came upon an subterranean realm verging on the fantastic.

Moricz stated that when he was a newly-arrived emigre in Argentina, he ran across an old man who told him about the "lost treasure of Atahualpa" and how it had been concealed by his followers in a series of subterranean cities. Fired by this knowledge, young Moricz decided to cross the breadth of Argentina until he reached the Andes and headed northward to where the mighty South American mountain range gives birth to the Amazon's headwaters.

In a scene straight out of Spielberg's "Raiders of the Lost Ark", Moricz came across tribes of fearsome Jívaro headhunters who are openly hostile to all outsiders. But rather than ending up another shrunken head, he discovered that he could make himself understood to the Jívaros by addressing them in his native Magyar! While this alone might strain anyone's suspension of disbelief, the fact remains that Moricz was able to live among the Jívaros long enough to learn their ways and make an important discovery: the jungle natives had peculiar dotted tattoos across their faces, centered on both cheeks, the chin and the nose. One day, he came across two Jívaro sentries guarding a boulder covered in the same design as the natives wore on their faces. Beyond the rock lay a narrow cave, and the explorer knew that he'd come across the access to the alleged lost hoard.

But the Jívaros cautioned him against entering, stating that the "dwellers in the depths" were gods endowed with beams capable of killing intruders and cutting through stone. The natives insisted on having seen the ground split open and produce brilliant balls of light that would rise heavenward.

Moricz decided that he was willing to place his life in jeopardy merely to see this fabled underground realm. He ventured into the cave, and then down some sort of chimney formation, leading to a slanted corridor made of perfectly dressed, angular stone. His wanderings eventually brought him to a chamber that was "perfectly lit by a quartz column" and from which many other hallways radiated.

Following one of them, Moricz came to a hall with a large circular table of polished stone, surrounded by seven stone seats. The walls were so highly polished as to be mirrored. Dubbing it "The Hall of the Seven Elders", the explorer pressed on, entering a series of narrow hallways which were as filthy as the earlier chambers had been clean. By now tired and forlorn from his meandering in this series of forgotten galleries, he was most startled to come across a cascade of greenish-blue water which appeared to be self luminous. His heart sank upon realizing that it had reached the end of the tunnels.

Suddenly — he told Del Amo-Freixedo — it occurred to him to go under the cascade and see if anything lay beyond. He was rewarded by brilliant sunlight and a sort of "terrace" looking down at the jungle canopy, hundreds of feet below. A narrow ledge led him to a large flat stone and the urge to "dig under it with his bare hands" to move it. Succeeding in this attempt, he reentered a series of ascending and descending passageways which ended in a vast chamber whose size he estimated at five hundred meters long by four hundred meters wide. The contents of this gargantuan hall — piles of gold, skeletons clad in unusual golden armor — appeared to be its source of illumination.

And it is here where Moricz already incredible story becomes fantastic: at the end of this "treasure chamber" were five creatures clad in metallic garments and having egg-shaped heads with large slanted black eyes. Their hair was held by a emerald-bearing band. "Your boldness has led you to where you are now," one of them reportedly said. "We have allowed you to reach us."

The creature then expounded on the catastrophes that had destroyed the surface races and how the entire history of their species was kept on gold-leafed books. He was then told to turn back and return to his people, but not to touch anything. "If you do, you will never return to the surface," they cautioned.

Many experts have written off Moricz's exploits as "tall tales" in the best tradition of Baron Munchausen, and cite his collaboration with Erich Von Daniken in The Gold of the Gods as proof of Moricz's nearly bottomless "private stock". It is up to the reader to decide.

The Central American

Tunnels Explored

But even if we should choose to dismiss

the adventures of Juan Moricz as merely fanciful, it by no means discredits the existence of the subterranean galleries.

In 1985, Spain's eminent UFO researcher, J.J. Benítez, joined the late Andreas Faber Kaiser and brothers Carlos and Ricardo Vílchez in exploring a series of clearly artificial tunnels which were not in the Andes, but in the Central American republic of Costa Rica.

According to the story, a Costa Rican family had learned many years ago that there was an ancient tunnel—located on the top of a nameless hill—which very possibly lead to an underground city. The family sold all of its belongings and literally "took to the hills", engaging in amateur excavations which resulted in the discovery of the opening to the tunnel. They found a shaft which dropped almost vertically and constituted the access to a corridor of dressed stone.

Members of the anonymous family group approached investigator Benítez and urged him to take a look. Accompanied by his fellow researchers, Benítez descended by means of rickety ladder and found himself staring at vast cyclopean blocks—carefully dressed and placed with almost geometric succession. At the end of the gallery, a side wall revealed a curious inscription written in an unknown language.

Subsequent linguistic research by Prof. Jesús Conte revealed that the curious inscription in the forgotten Costa Rican tomb was very similar to ancient Assyrian script [my italics]. Prof. Conte's painstaking analysis disclosed that the characters stated: "Beware! Impending Disaster!"

No good reason has been offered for the discovery of proto-Assyrian text in a cyclopean gallery fifty meters beneath the earth in Costa Rica, thousands of miles from the Middle East. Benítez speculates that this proto-Assyrian may have indeed been the language spoken on Atlantis and which later survived in the Fertile Crescent. If Benítez's suppositions are on target, the reader can well imagine what impeding disaster was being referred to.

Stories of networks of artificially created tunnels riddling the five continents are certainly nothing new: adventure writers of the '30s waxed eloquent on the supposed tunnels in Central Asia which linked a number of cave systems to the mystical realm of Agharta, or the tunnels beneath Lhasa's Potala temple linking it to other lamaseries in the Himalayas; the connectivity between the cave systems of the Rocky Mountains is also well-known. But we needn't strap on our headlamps and go spelunking just yet—a fully electrified and technological subterranean "culture" was discovered in 1993 in Northern Italy.

A Number Of Mexican Oddities

Mexico offers its own share of subterranean mysteries. Foremost among these is the "sunken palace" of Dzibilchaltún.

In 1941, a group of teenagers bathing in one of the Yucatan Peninsula's many limestone cenotes, was startled to discover that behind the jungle thickness that surrounded their favorite bathing spot was a wall of dressed stone. They notified the authorities, which in turn advised the Secretariat of Education. Faced with the prospect of cleaning up this twenty square mile area, containing approximately four hundred structures, the Mexican government turned to the Middle American Research Institute at the University of New Orleans, which would in coming years begin exploring the ruins of Dzibilchaltún — the name given by an old Maya shaman, who informed them that the word was not of Mayan origin. However, the lagoon near the ruins had a clearly Mayan denomination: Xlacah, "the old city".

The archaeologists were clearly mystified by this denomination, and suspecting that the old shaman was making reference to some sort of acropolis, requested more information. They were then regaled with the story of how in ages past, a massive palace had once occupied the area—the home of Dzibilchaltún's ruler— and how one day a stranger had appeared at the palace gate, requesting shelter. The ruler ordered his servants to prepare lodging for the unexpected guest. The following day, in exchange for the cacique's hospitality, the strange traveller produced a large green gem from his satchel and turned it over to the ruler, who soon turned greedy and asked the stranger if his satchel contained even more treasures. When the stranger refused to answer, he was summarily executed by the guards and the satchel was handed to the ruler, who was disappointed to find in it only some travel-stained garments and a large black stone. In rage, the cacique hurled the black stone out a window: it struck the ground with a tremendous explosion, causing the palace and its occupants to slide into the newly created hole.

It wasn't until 1961 that archaeologists would brave the depths of Xlacah: their exploration of the muddy cenote proved that the limestone structure was shaped like a boot and extended to a depth that was hard to fathom. Upon reaching the end of the vertical segment, they found the remains of the "sunken palace"'s columns and adorned walls.

Hot Times Under Moscow

There are, of course, individuals who remain skeptical to any notion of subterranean occupancy of our world—that goes beyond provisional shelters and subway stations—indicating the difficulty in providing ventilation, temperature control and sanitation for any permanent underground tenancy, particularly one involving tens of thousands of people.

However, the prestigious Bulletin of Atomic Scientists (May/June 1997) presented an extraordinary article involving the existence of multiple subterranean tiers under the city of Moscow. Following the adventures of Vadim Mikhailov and his group "Diggers of the Underground Planet", the BAS article reveals the shadowy underworld of the Russian capital: The Diggers made their way through fallout shelters to a colossal warehouse owned by a Russian marine biology institution, containing among other nightmarish holdings "a room of tanks of formalin, containing various sea monsters."

After well over a decade of urban spelunking, the Diggers have presented the world with a map of the nightmarish that occupies these levels: gypsies, malcontents, dissidents and "professional hermits" have occupied the levels closest to the surface, gaining access through heating vents and sewer systems. On one particular journey deep under the Centrobank building, the Diggers encountered squads of uniformed people lighting their way with powerful halogen lamps. The authorites dismissed the explorers' claims as fanciful, but the BAS article quotes Mikhailov as saying that the authorities in fact have no idea who these armed, masked individuals could be, and insist that the security services themselves do not venture down to those levels.

At even greater depths under the city, Mikhailov's group encountered stranger things, such as mass burial sites from an unknown age, ancient weapons similar to maces; a "secret" railway system built under Stalin and never used by the public; deserted laboratories with outdated equipment and intriguing flasks, and perhaps more interestingly, a bunker able to hold thousands of people beneath the location of a demolished cathedral. According to Mikhailov, the dean of the Cathedral of Christ the Savior approached him with a request to enter the area and remove a strange container that even filled the dean with terror. Under the Skliffasovsky Clinic, the urban spelunkers ran into a strange cult in monkish robes, circumambulating around a stone altar. The monk-like figures ran away upon being seen by the explorers.

The Diggers have since engaged in what could well be considered their most important quest: the resting place of the trove of manuscripts brought from Constantinople to Moscow in the 15th century by Sophia Palaeologus as part of her dowry. This collection of priceless texts is reputedly safeguarded by paranormal forces which have caused misfortunes to those seeking them.

Underground Realms Here And Now

Bruno Tinti, district attorney of the northern Italian city of Ivrea, did not believe at first the reports of a lost and magical city in the foothills of the Piedmont. In a country racked by extremist terrorism, Tinti took no chances: he promptly dispatched a regiment of Carabineri, who would later confirm the city's existence. Not far from the town of Baldissero Canavavese, near the city of Turin, a secret entrance leads to the thirty meter depth where the occult community of Damanhur thrives. A seemingly endless maze of temples, labyrinths and meeting halls, decorated with Ancient Egyptian and esoteric symbols, Damanhur boasts inordinate wealth: the floors and walls of its chambers are covered in marble, gold, mosaics and mirrors worthy of the grandest European palaces.

Founded in 1975 by Oberto Airuldi, the earthmoving activities which led to the creation of the subterranean city were financed by the 300 members of Damanhur's "Council of Elders"—captains of industry and commerce whose activities net them an combined income of over $8 million dollars per annum. Damanhur is a fully independent state, with its own government, constitution and minted coinage. Although its inhabitants resented the intrusion of the police authorities, they are reportedly secretly pleased that word of their hidden city has reached the outside world.

Damanhur consists of five temples linked by a number of passageways; it's stonework is so elaborate that it has reminded many of that of the Egyptian great pyramid, and others of the heliolithic ruins on the island of Malta. The Damanhurians (for want of a better name) have an interesting and progressive social system in which human initiative and freewill are considered of paramount importance, as well as the role of the individual over that of the family. Marriage vows are reconfirmed every three years and as in most utopian societies, children are raised in common by the community and taught how to solve problems and glean information using both hemispheres of the brain.

The five temples of subterranean Damanhur represent the culmination of the Damanhurians secret lore. Allegedly, each temple represents one of the four elements (air, water, earth and fire) and the fifth temple is forbidden to outsiders. According to the fortunate few who have been invited to this subterranean empire, the temple of air is completely covered in mirrors and surmounted by a depiction of the universe and the temple of earth contains under its dome the largest stained glass image ever built by man.

Conclusion

The existence of Damanhur points to the

human need to build subterranean structures for a variety of esoteric and exoteric reasons. The avowed purpose of this magical city in the Italian piedmont is to preserve man's occult and alchemical knowledge—can we not assume that earlier human civilizations may have felt a similar impulse on the genetic level to "preserve" the best of their achievements for their descendants many aeons into the future? What if a catastrophe changed the face of Europe, and in a few centuries skeptics scoffed at the existence of a "Damanhur" and its works? Are we not doing the same with all these other locations that lore and human endeavor have been made known to us? Places like Chincana, the unplumbed tunnels of the Andes, mysterious Moscow, and many others possibly contain the legacies of our forerunners. We are morally bound to find them.

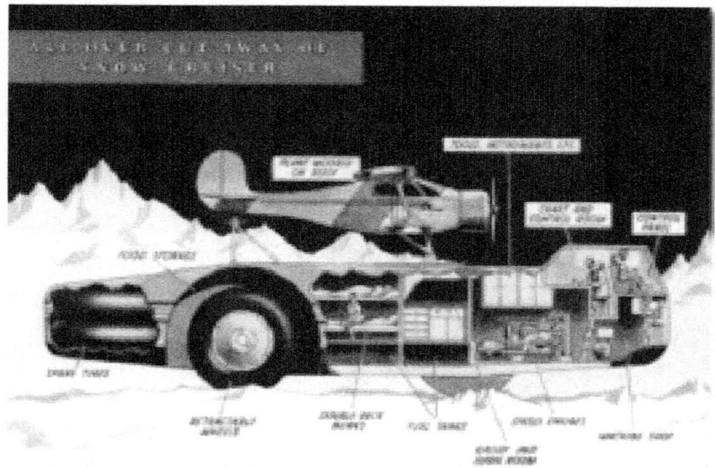

Antarctic Snow Cruiser on W. Wyandot Ave. in Upper Sandusky, Ohio on November 1, 1939. English Lutheran church behind Cruiser cab.

DEUTSCHE ANTARKTISCHE EXPEDITION
NEU-SCHWABENLAND
20 0 20
SÜDPOL
1938-1939

Why Were The Nazi War Machine And The U. S. Waging An All Out Battle To Get To The Poles First?

By Dennis Crenshaw

In early 1938 those in the know were well aware that a war was on the horizon in Europe. The German leader Adolf Hitler was beginning to flex his muscles as he launched a massive expansion of Germany's borders. On September 23rd Charles A. Lindbergh, who had been living abroad since the kidnapping and murder of his infant son in 1932, wrote a letter to the United States Ambassador to Britain, Joseph Kennedy, in which he stated:*I am convinced that it is wiser to permit Germany eastward expansion than to throw England and France, unprepared, into a war at this time. Britain cannot win a war in Europe even with U.S. aid.*(4).

Germany had been bankrupt since 1931 and their trade balance showed a trade deficit of 432 million marks.(5) and expansion and buildup of war materials was putting additional strain on Hitler's pocketbook. The financial woes were all pushed aside to finance an expensive expedition that was then in the planning stages. An expedition that was important to the Nazi hierarchy for reasons which have been kept secret till this very day.

On a winter night in 1938 the German research ship *Schwabenland* cast off from a dock in Hamburg - destination Antarctica. Aboard, accompanying the ships hand-picked crew was some of Germany's top airmen, technicians, oceanographers, biologists, meteorologist and earth scientists, all members of the First Deutsche Antarktische Expedition of 1938-1939. The people who made up the costly Antarctic expedition were under secret orders not to divulge their mission, the purpose of which little is known today.

Enter Admiral Richard E. Byrd

On *Saturday July 8th, 1939* Americans across the country opened their morning newspaper to a front-page story not unlike the one from *The New York Times* Quoted below.

President Directs Speed on Byrd Trip

(Excerpts)

WASHINGTON, July 7 — *President Roosevelt moved today to prevent possible extension of Germany's claims to Antarctic areas into the Western Hemisphere by directing Real Admiral Richard E. Byrd to leave in October to territory within the sphere of influence of the Monroe Doctrine. It [is] apparent that this government was prepared to take the position, if necessary, that any attempts by foreign powers to establish bases west of the 180th meridian in the Antarctic would be considered an unfriendly act. If the $340,000 appropriated by Congress for the expedition permitted, Admiral Byrd said, he would outfit three ships. His own ship would be The Bear of Oakland, which is undergoing a careful inspection at Boston. He said he would lend it to the government after a new engine had been installed.*

As we can see from the above a major confrontation between American and German forces seemed to be a very real and present danger in Antarctica in 1939.

However, in retrospect we find that, though the German presence in the "land of everlasting mystery" was the publicized reason for Admiral Byrd's hurry-up expedition, at no time did Admiral Byrd or those under his command make any attempt to observe what the German expedition was up to. In fact a look at the map on page 111 of *Cristof Friedrich's* well documented study of the German expedition, *Germany's Antarctic Claim: Secret Nazi Polar Expeditions* will show that neither in the 1938 - 39 nor the subsequent 1947 and 1955 expeditions to Antarctica did the Americans come anywhere close to the lands claimed by the Germans. Could the stated reason for the 1939 expedition, as is often the case in military operations, only a cover for a more "important" secret mission for Admiral Byrd and his fellow members of the 1939 expedition. The following small article, hidden away on a back page of the *November 30th, 1939* issue of *The New York Times,* highlights that possibility.

Secret Orders Taken

By Byrd On Polar Trip

(Excerpts)

WASHINGTON, Nov. 29 (AP) — *Rear Admiral Richard E. Byrd joined the vanguard of his South Pole expedition at the Panama Canal today with confidential orders from the White House. Officials say the Orders were a State Department secret. ... Even the existence of the orders, authorities said, had been kept secret ...Admiral Byrd received them, informants say, on a hurried trip to Washington last week before departing for Panama.*

Is it possible that these "secret orders" contained the real reason for Admiral Byrd's expedition? And was the facts that the Germans were also conducting a "secret" expedition in Antarctica make the Admiral's real reason for putting together the American expedition a matter of upmost importance? Could both expeditions have been carrying secret orders to explore "unknown lands beyond the pole?" Were the Americans and Germans involved, in 1939, in a race to be the first to gain entrance, and explore the legendary lands inside our earth? A race not unlike the "space race" between America and Russia several decades later. In an upcoming issue we will look into this possibility, but for now let's look at another mystery.

As I stated in *THEI, Volume 1* if you are going to explore unknown lands the first thing you must have is a base camp, or "Last Outpost," on the edge of the area you wish to explore. Here you would store your supplies, maintain medical facilites and pitch your radio tent so the exploring teams could keep in contact. That camp was already in place. In January of 1929 Admiral Byrd established Little America as that outpost on the Antarctic continent.

But what if the area to be explored wasn't a barren land of ice and snow? What if it were more supportive of life than we are told - such as unknown, thought-to-be extinct huge wild animals and reptiles, and even more dangerous, creatures of intelligence equal or greater than mans? In that case the best piece of equipment to have would be some sort of mobile base. One that would enable your expedition crews a way to cover a lot of territory very quickly, and at the same time, be a haven of relative safety for the adventuresome explorers.

The Mysterious Snow Cruiser Front-page story of *July 8th 1939*, *The New York Times*:

Snow Cruiser

Offered By the Associated Press

WASHINGTON, July 7 - *A giant 'Snow Cruiser' specially designed to span yawning crevasses and jagged ice ridges, may be a major piece of equipment on the Byrd expedition. The cruiser was designed by Dr. Thomas C. Pouiter of Chicago, second-in-command of the Byrd expedition in 1933-35.*

In recent testimony before a House appropriations subcommittee he indicated that the odd craft could carry sufficient equipment for an exploring party to last a year.

On its deck, Dr. Pouiter suggested, the machine could carry a Navy pursuit plane, which by making short flights at 300-mile intervals, could explore about 5,000 square miles of unknown territory during a single

Antarctic summer. (Underline added - Editor).

Let's stop and let that sink in. *Sufficient equipment for an exploring party to last a year! Could explore 5 hundred thousand miles of unknown territory.* That's a lot of ice and snow to say the least. Put into perspective that is equal to *one hundred auto trips from Anchorage Alaska to Jacksonville Florida!* Someone was planning an expedition that, in its time, seems to rival man's first trip to the moon. Naturally something of this magnitude was destined to capture the interest of the press and the citizens of America. The step by step development of this 'snow cruiser' was followed eagerly by the media of the day. From the *July 15th 1939* issue of *The New York Times*:

Byrd to Use Army Tanks on Polar Quest; Big Snow Cruiser in Antarctic Equipment

By The Associated Press

(Excerpts).

BOSTON, July 14 - *Rear Admiral Richard E. Byrd disclosed plans for his coming ex-*

pedition in the Antarctic said today that 6 army tanks and a unique 45,000 pound snow cruiser would be used for transport over the South Pole's icy wastelands ... The snow cruiser ... would carry four men and a plane, and would be extremely mobile and easy to manipulate under the difficult conditions found in Antarctica.

I found the next significant mention of the 'snow cruiser' in *the August 2, 1939* issue of *The New York Times* in, of all places, The Society Section:

Giant Tire Soon Ready Made in Akron for Antarctic Trip

It Will Weigh 1,900 Pounds

CHICAGO, Aug. 1 (AP) - *The Armor Institute of Technology said today that the first of the giant tires for the ice cruiser of the government's coming Arctic expedition would be taken from its mold at the Goodyear Tire and Rubber Company's plant at Akron Aug. 9.*

Harold Vagtborg, director of the Armor Foundation, said the 10-foot tire, each weighing 1,900 pounds, will be the largest ever manufactured.

Not to be outdone, many of the nationally read popular magazines of the time also ran their own stories, complete with drawings and diagrams of the giant vehicle. *Scientific American* ran their story in the January 1940 issue. However they were beaten to the punch by *Popular Mechanics* whose story *Snow Cruiser to Explore Antarctic* was featured in their October 1939 issue. According to their report the huge monster vehicle designed to *climb the polar mountains and slither across giant crevasses* would be fifty-five feet long and fifteen feet wide.

The power would be supplied by two 200-hp diesel engines that would be connected to generators *to furnish power for driving, for radio, electronic stoves, heat and the machine shop.* The giant cruiser would be controlled by one man who would be in the 'second floor' cabin. The *Popular Mechanics* article continued to describe the vehicle.

Below [the driver] is the repair shop; to the rear, navigation chart desk, galley which *is also photographic darkroom, bunkroom, storeroom and a compartment in the tail for two spare tires. The cruiser will have a 5,000-mile range, and will travel at from ten to thirty miles an hour under any conditions except severe blizzards. An automatic gyro-pilot may be installed to hold the cruiser on any course set. Front and rear wheels steer independently so that the Antarctic bus can turn in a thirty-degree radius or shift sideways at a twenty-five degree angle. The scientists will measure thickness of the ice with the geophysical seismograph, make gravity determinations and meteorological observations, survey unexplored Antarctica and study the Aurora, Terrestrial magnetism, meteors and other phenomena. Cruiser and equipment will cost $150,000.* [1939 Dollars.]

The *Popular Mechanics* article also reported that the Navy BI-plane which *carried a seven-inch lens mapping camera*, was rigged atop the cruiser in such a way as to be *hauled to its perch by winch or launched on the snow in ten minutes.*

As the planners moved full-bore ahead

with their plans the public was taken along for the trip through the pages of newspapers across the nation. On October 15th *the New York Times* ran a picture of the partially completed cruiser along with an article titled:

Byrd Expedition Gets Polar Gear

Two ships and 125 Men, 160 Dogs and5,000 Varied Items are going to Antarctic

Five Planes to Be Taken

3 Tanks and a Snowmobile Are to Aid Work. Departure Set for Early Next Month

BOSTON, Oct. 14 (UP) - *The greatest Antarctic expedition in history — both in numbers and accessories is being assembled here for what may be a tortoise-like race with Nazi scientists for* [mineral] *rich south polar areas.*

A century after the first United States Antarctic expedition, this second government-financed group will be directed by Real Admiral Richard E. Byrd, who twice in the last decade has led his own expeditions into the

land where nights are four months long.

Delayed a month, the expedition hopes to leave Nov. 1, reaching its destination when harbors are ice-free and if possible ahead of parties reportedly organizing in Germany and other countries.

Once finished the snow cruiser was driven from the factory in Chicago to the dock in Boston supported by a police escort that halted traffic along the highways in 20-mile stretches so the huge machine could pass. Thousands of people followed its progress in newspaper articles and radio reports. Many stopped along the route, or made a special trip, to try and catch a glimpse of the giant machine.

By October 28, 1939 the cruiser was well on its way to Boston, but not without mishap. From the October 29th, 1939 issue of *The New York Times;*

Byrd Snow Craft Founders in Creek

35-ton 60-Foot Cruiser Hits an Ohio Bridge and Plunges off Road into Water

(Excerpts)

Lima, Ohio, Oct. 28 (UP) - *The giant snow cruiser struck a bridge near Gomer, about 10 miles from here and stumbled into a stream ... The machine drove its nose several feet below the surface of the water while the rest of it was left spanning the stream ... it [will] be several days before the huge machine could be raised from Pine Run Creek and the trip resumed ...*

Everywhere it traveled the strange-looking vehicle made headlines. *The New York Times,* November 1939,

Byrd's Snow Cruiser Startles

Bay Traffic

Snarls Traffic in Crawling over

The Berkshires

Special to *The New York Times*

Boston, Mass. Nov, 13 - *The Antarctic snow cruiser, most tenacious road hog ever to invade New England, steering a leisurely, bouncing course today over the Berkshires from Pittsfield to Farmington, caused the greatest traffic jam in Massachusetts history*

One letter to the editor, obviously from someone who had been caught up in the movement of the huge craft halfway across America, published in the November 14th 1939, *The New York Times* stated that the snow cruiser ... *is a thing that has to be seen to be believed. Once seen, it makes one happy as well as proud to know that it soon will be traveling the Antarctic Continent, where it cannot hold up 70,000 motor cars and create a 90-mile traffic jam, as it did in Massachusetts on Sunday. ...*

Then on November 15th 1939 *The New York Times* headline many had been waiting for:

Cruiser Aboard, Byrd Ship to Sail; Snowmobile is lashed to deck; And North Star Prepares to Leave Boston at Dawn Today

Expedition Chief Proposes Ice Habitation for 5 or 6 Years to Clinch Discovery Claims

[Note headline above ... Byrd was planning *a 5 or 6 year habitation* "to Clinch Discovery Claims"... or was the "exploration" with the snow cruiser which was equipped with a year's provisions for its on-board crew expected to bring back new" discoveries" ... possable "discoveries" the NAZIs were also after.

In January 1940, as reported in the January 19th issue of *The New York Times,* the closely watched, well-documented cruiser arrived in Antarctica:

Snow Cruiser Road Test

Byrd Cruiser in Antarctic Crash

Special to the *New York Times (Excerpts)* Washington, Jan 18 - *A narrow escape from disaster in moving the Byrd Antarctic snow cruiser from the ship to the ice at the expeditions landing place in the Bay of Whales. Amid a welter of flying splinters and broken planks, the gigantic snow cruiser lumbered safely ashore tonight from the Antarctic Service ship North Star. The cruiser ... Kept on the move once all four of her ten-foot wheels reached treacherous bay ice alongside the ship. Remaining at the controls, Dr. Thomas C. Pouiter of Chicago drove her a full mile from the ship before coming to a halt. ...*

As we can see from the documentation in the report, the Snow Cruiser was the star of Admiral Byrd's 1939 Antarctic Expedition. For months Americans had read every tiny detail about the progress of manufacturing the beast. The delivery was like the coming of the circus parade and that close enough, or lucky enough, to travel to the publicized route lined the highways as the celebrated vehicle passed by. In fact the snow machine was featured in every newspaper headline concerning the preparations for the 1939 Antarctic Expedition. But it wasn't until after the 'outpost on wheels' was reported to have made it safely to the Mysterious Continent the mystery begins.

I have spent many, many hours searching through back issues of newspaper and magazine indexes after that final report. Nothing. Once again, as with every investigation into Admiral Byrd's shenanigans in the Polar Regions of our globe, a lead I was following had vanished like a puff of smoke. It was as though the snow cruiser never existed. What happened to the monster machine and the data it was designed to gather? Could it and a handpicked crew, once unloaded, have gone off on a mission of their own? A mission so secret that it has not been talked about even to this day. There is an official explanation. The Snow Cruiser failed to perform in the snow so they would have us believe that it was simply abandoned.

Our final newspaper article might hold a couple of clues. The May 15th issue of *The New York Times* carried a lengthy article detailing Admiral Byrd's report on the findings of the 1939 United States Antarctic Service Expedition. The Admiral reported that the expedition achieved much more than he thought possible, including *the discovery of 900 miles of unknown coastline that explorers had been seeking for a hundred years.*

In the lengthy interview he never mentioned the snow cruiser. Even stranger, was that apparently he was never asked. The giant machine that had been on every one's minds and lips before Byrd left might never had existed. He did tell us *that 59 men were left behind to carry on*. Were these brave souls the crew and support team for a secret mission using the mighty cruiser to explore "the lands beyond the poles?"

The article also tells us that The Admiral emphasized the fact that this was not "another Byrd expedition" but "a project sponsored by the United States Government." In other words John D. Rockefeller and his pals didn't foot the bill this time ... Uncle Sam did i.e. the United States taxpayers. He ended the interview with the statement that henceforth he will direct the expedition from Washington.

What expedition? The "official" expedition was over. And what about the *59 men left behind to carry on.* Are these small clues pointing towards a longer secret mission to explore for rumored habitable lands somewhere in the polar region? Is it true what many have said all along? Did Admiral Byrd dedicate his life to locating and exploring lands inside our earth with entrances at the poles? Was this expedition and the 'outpost on wheels' a step closer towards achieving Admiral Byrd's goal? Is the existence of polar openings which can be used to access interior lands truly the **"Closest Guarded Secret in the World?"**

Sources

Newspaper source: *the New York Times* Books & Articles;

(1) *Beyond the Barrier,* Page XI, Eugene Rogers, Naval Institute Press: Annapolis, Maryland. 1990.

(2) Rear Admiral Byrd and the Polar Expeditions, Page 99, Coram Foster, A.L. Burt Co: N.Y. 1930.

(3) *Beyond the Barrier*. Pages 274-275.

(4) *The People's Chronology*, Page 852, James Trager, Henry Holt: N.Y. 1992

(5) *Ibid*. Page 853.

(6) Germany's Antarctic Claim: Secret Polar Expeditions, Christof Friedrich: Samisdat Press: Toronto, Canada. 1977

Brooks Agnew – Scientist

In Search of Hollow Earth Reality

By Tim R. Swartz

Brooks A. Agnew, PhD, is a commercial scientist and engineer with more than 17 years of field research in Earth Tomography. He also has 15 years of experience creating more than $500 million in process improvements for numerous industries.

His patents have revolutionized photopolymer applications, digital imaging, and high-speed manufacturing processes creating more than five thousand jobs. His technology is used on at least two planets to explore for water and other compounds.

Raised in Pasadena, California, Dr.

Agnew spent most of his youth hanging around Cal Tech and the folks who worked at the Jet Propulsion Labs. He entered the Air Force in 1973 where he became an electronics engineer. After earning an honorable discharge he attended Brigham Young, Western Kentucky, and Tennessee Technological Universities.

Dr. Agnew has a BS Degree in Chemistry, an MS Degree in Statistics, and a PhD in Physics. He also graduated as class valedictorian in Entrepreneurial Studies and produced a training video on raising money for non-profit ventures.

As a commercial scientist, he has produced thousands of technical papers and numerous patents. He was a featured scientist in the video documentary on ***HAARP: Holes in Heaven***, directed by Emmy Award Winning Wendy Robbins. He recently coauthored the two national best selling volumes of ***The Ark of Millions of Years.***

Dr. Agnew has recently received substantial attention from the press because of his planned expedition to the Arctic, North Pole Inner Earth Expedition (NPIEE), to hopefully discover the Northern Polar opening to the hollow Earth. The Kentucky based physicist and futurist hopes to board the commercially owned Russian ice-breaker Yamal in the port of Murmansk, and to sail into the polar sea just beyond Canada's Arctic islands.

Dr. Agnew is the latest in a long line of people to examine the theory that humans live on the surface of a hollow planet, in which two undiscovered openings, near the North and South poles, connect the outer Earth with an interior realm. However, the original idea to mount a modern-day quest for the Polar opening belongs to the late Steve Currey, a Utah adventure guide who organized rafting trips to the world's wildest white-water rivers. Currey knew how to hype exotic destinations and recruit would-be explorers on trips of a lifetime.

Currey pinpointed the Arctic opening at 84.4 degrees north and 41 degrees east, roughly 250 miles northwest of Ellesmere Island. The inner Earth expedition was scheduled for the summer of 2006, with spaces offered for $20,000.

When Currey died unexpectedly of brain cancer, Dr. Agnew stepped in to take his place. The trip was postponed and, while he insists the journey has a genuine scientific purpose, Dr. Agnew also says the expedition will include several experts in meditation, mythology and UFOs, as well as a team of documentary filmmakers.

However, if nothing is found, Dr. Agnew still promises a grand polar adventure, no matter what the outcome.

"If the polar opening isn't there, the voyage will still make an outstanding documentary," he says. "But if we do find something, this will be the greatest geological discovery in the history of the world."

Dr. Agnew says that much of the Arctic area of planet Earth has never been seen or properly analyzed by humans. Utilizing leading-edge science such as side-scan sonar, dynamo sensing, and gyroscopic global circumference tracking, the team expects to precisely measure the crust and the ocean's physical properties to reveal unprecedented features about our planet. Sea-water chemistry, marine life cataloging, and even magnetic measurements will be collected during the 13-day expedition to see if there is any hard evidence that might support the hollow Earth hypothesis.

Now, no experiment on this subject would be complete without the other components so vehemently demanded by millions of paranormal prognosticators. There is a multidimensional aspect to this subject matter.

Many believe that there is a void in the interior of the Earth, but that it is fourth, and perhaps even fifth dimensional. These dimensions may require the observer to access higher vibrational levels than the vast sea of seeing-is-believing folks that clog our freeways. There will also be observation effects from the very measurement of these never before seen regions of planet Earth. Something or someone might be disturbed by this process. In other words, if the side-scan sonar sends a pulse across the bow of a 200-foot ship peacefully parked on the floor of the 4200-meter deep ocean, it might relocate itself. Besides being graphed by the sonar software, when that craft moves someone is going to get that movement on film.

QUESTIONS AND ANSWERS WITH BROOK AGNEW

Q: What is your background (education, profession, interests)?

Agnew: I was sort of a permanent student from 1970 until 2000 when I completed my PhD. I started out working as a lab assistant at UCLA Brain Research Institute while my brother was working on his PhD. I have been involved with science or engineering every since. I got my bachelor's degree from Tennessee Technological University in Chemistry. I went to work full time to support my family and worked through the Masters and Doctoral programs using extension and online courses.

My main interest has been manufacturing systems. I have worked for nearly every major auto maker in the U.S., as well as numerous suppliers for the industry. I am a certified quality engineer with a Black

Belt in Six-Sigma quality systems.

I co-authored a book on the creation of the Earth in 2005, called ***The Ark of Millions of Years***, which rapidly became a national best seller. I began doing radio interviews by demand, and soon was asked to host my own radio program. I founded X-Squared Radio in 2005 and have been growing every since with that wonderful hobby on the BBS Radio Network. We are modeled after Coast-to-Coast AM, but have a distinctly scientific theme with the best guests on Earth.

Q: How did you get interested in the hollow Earth theory?

Agnew: I joined the Inner Earth Expedition in 2005 as a team member to build a gyroscope and help with water sampling and analysis. I was happy to be part of the team. Steven Currey tragically and unexpectedly passed away in the summer of 2006, and I was elected to be the project leader.

Our team looked at the most likely way to fund a $2 million expedition and figured that a documentary film would be the best bet. We did not want to make the film the goal, but then again the world would probably best experience the expedition through film. We calculated that someone with financial backing would see the same incredible value that we did. So far, it has worked out that way.

Q: There is a long history on the idea that the Earth could be hollow, is there any modern science that could suggest the reality of the hollow Earth?

Agnew: The history of the hollow Earth is certainly fascinating and entertaining, but until recently lacked any credible scientific data to back it up. Satellite photos of the Earth have allowed the formation of serious questions and thus hypothesis to be formed about the structure of the planet.

Two things in particular showed up. The first was a photo of the Aurora Borealis over both planetary poles at the same time. This virtually ruled out the idea that this particular phenomenon was caused by the solar wind, a previously assumed source. Second, the USGS seismic data repeatedly, for more than 600,000 reports, produced data inconsistent with the current plate tectonic theory.

Q: Seismic research has shown anomalies that some scientists say could indicate a crust of 800 to 900 miles thick with an open area and then possibly a core of hot iron/nickel – how is this type of research done and who has made these suggestions?

Agnew: When the seismic data is recalculated, using the accelerometer as the starting point and the point of Earthquake as the endpoint, the results are stunning. A clear picture of a planet with a 900 mile thick crust appears in the math models. This, coupled with Washington University study by Dr. Wysessions, produced evidence that another entire ocean may exist underneath the Atlantic Ocean.

There is more. The magnetosphere around Earth is generated by a counter-rotation between two metal bodies. The first is the crust, which is now three times its original post-accretion disc diameter.

The second is the iron core, which was

left behind during the overspin condition once the Earth began cooling. The crust is still in a slow expansion, filling with molten magma where the openings to the magma below are formed. By now, as the reader might notice, the crust is stable and cool enough to support liquid water and thus life.

Q: There have been astronomical observations that suggest the Earth is not alone in being hollow. Is there any theory that could explain how the Earth, and other planets, could form with a hollow center?

Agnew: The prevailing theory is that planets form from large accretion discs. These are huge slowly spinning discs of dust and rock. As this mini-galaxy of material becomes attracted to the center, planets begin to form. The Newtonian idea that mass attracts mass, through his concept of gravitation, denotes that in the center, the largest mass collects where the centrifugal forces are weakest. The gravity is believed to be enough to generate enough crushing power to light off the sun.

Now, as we zoom into a single planet, we

see a really interesting dynamic process. The dust and rock coagulates into a single body. Obeying the law of conservation of momentum, this little rock spins faster and faster as it gets smaller. We have evidence that one of three things happens.

First, the planet can spin so fast that it explodes. The evidence of this is the plethora of asteroids and free-floating planets we have observed. Second, the planet can spin fast enough to throw off a chunk of itself. This usually exists as a moon. Sometimes that moon can be small enough to stay in orbit, and sometimes it is large enough that it breaks off and forms its own orbit around the central sun. We have evidence of both in our own solar system. Of course, we observe dozens of moons in our own solar system. And, Venus' moon broke off and became Mercury.

The third condition is the gray area in between these two extremes. The crust expands through upheavals, thinning, and cracking. The force releases in the form of heat which melts the inner layers to magma under extreme stress. As the crust cracks open, the magma flows to the outside, cools, and cements the crust back together.

We have clear evidence of this as rock assumes the planet's magnetic alignment at the instant it cools. As the crust expands, the alignment shifts. We have observed igneous rock with a gradient of magnetic fields. This could very well support this theory of crustal expansion.

Why is this important? Because if the crust is expanding, there is another interesting dynamic happening below; let's throw in an Einstein idea here. Suppose you were standing on a bathroom scale in an elevator. That elevator is a shaft that goes to the center of the Earth. When you press the button to go down, you observe your weight on the scale. Sure enough as you approach the center of the Earth, your weight begins to drop. Why? Because all of the mass of the Earth is above you in every direction; like standing on the North Pole, every direction is south.

Now, couple these ideas, and you will see why planets form as spheres and not as solid balls. The crust expands, leaving behind a molten ball of metal, probably iron. The crust is clearly three times its original size, as can be easily seen by fitting all the continental shelves together. The gap left behind is an open void. It is filled with air and water. We have historical evidence of cataclysmic periods when the interior of the Earth vented to the exterior of the Earth.

The idea that planets form as hollow spheres is scientifically plausible, but not generally canonized by the high priests of science. Hence, we are mounting an expedition to gather enough observational evidence to either refute or prove the theory.

Q: Why do you think that most geologists ignore such findings, preferring to "hang with the pack," refusing even to look at the evidence or speculate beyond the excepted theories of modern geology?

Agnew: It is not so much that they refuse to look at evidence. We have some of the best minds in the world joining our expedition. The problem exists because the approving authorities for PhD's are very conservative, but it goes beyond that. The previous degrees granted are based on things being a certain way. Upsetting that basis for "truth" negates all the previous degrees. In other words, if you got your PhD on the idea that Earth is flat and the sun revolved around the Earth, then sanctioning Galileo's ideas would put your tenure in question. No one wants to be the first to announce that heavier-than-air flight is now possible. Of course, that is irrelevant to those who are looking out the window of their aircraft at the degreed non-fliers below.

Q: What about the theorized holes at the poles? In this age of satellite photography and jetliners supposedly flying over the poles, how could something as obvious as polar openings be kept hidden?

Agnew: Actually, the evidence from both activities is lacking for two reasons. The first is the fact that polar satellites are looking at the Earth from about 260 miles away. They have visible, infrared, magnetic, and x-ray receivers. They are primarily used for weather reporting and thermal reviews of the Earth. The images of the poles don't really exist anymore. The Data Denial Act of 2006 prevents the release of data below 60 degrees latitude to the public. Google Maps animates their data above these areas.

The second reason is that the poles are almost always covered with clouds. This has been the main reason that there is still some credibility to Admiral Byrd's record-breaking polar flight. He flew at an altitude between 1,500 and 2,500 feet. At that altitude, your first mistake is your last.

However, Byrd very likely flew beneath the clouds giving him a clear view of the terrain below. He also would not have had the perspective to know that he was flying into an opening.

The apparent report that Admiral Byrd observed green grass, flowing water, and woolly mammoths where certainly none should have been was what really revived the age-old assertion that the Earth might be hollow. The modern plan to fly across the poles at low altitude is not practical. The cheapest aircraft that could make the

6,000 mile range is a Boeing 727. It would cost about $30,000 for such a trip. The major drawback is that no pilot is going to fly that aircraft for any period of time below 10 thousand feet in altitude. At that altitude, nothing would be visible except clouds.

Q: In your own opinion, do you think that past polar explorers encountered the openings or other anomalies associated with the polar openings?

Agnew: In my opinion, direct observation is excellent evidence. Scientifically speaking, lack of repeatability means the data is not legitimate. Edmund Haley was a strong advocate for the hollow Earth. He had very elaborate theories and great drawings of his ideas. In the 1830's another surge for the theory came out. We think it about time that someone went to the North Pole and gathered some real hard data and some really good film.

Q: Tell us about the upcoming Arctic trip that you are planning to try and find the Northern opening and other interesting mysteries.

Agnew: The expedition was originally planned by a group lead by Steven Currey. He had a good reputation for exotic and unusual expeditions. Tragically, he died during the preparation of this expedition. I was elected to be the new leader last October. The original funds collected were refunded by the Currey Estate, and we started over on funding.

The team consists of 100 experts in various fields. We are currently collecting scientists from major universities with expertise in polar research. We have signed experts in diving and arctic filmmaking. Then there is the Indiana Jones aspect of the expedition. In preparing for this trip, some rather powerful and esoteric events happened that convinced us there might be a higher-dimensional aspect to this entire venture. We were convinced, through various means, that we had to address these aspects or the expedition would fail.

Our leadership began training in meditation, light frequency and sound frequency chakra correlations, and even advanced physics for portal cognition. At long last, the project began moving forward extremely rapidly. The supporters for this project have come forth from every side. It seemed as though everyone got the message that we were somehow invited to visit this legendary opening. Perhaps there is an intelligence that knows we are coming and is paving the way and opening doors for us to get there.

There are two entities we have created to accomplish this voyage. The first is a non-profit company called Phoenix Science Foundation:

www.phoenixsciencefoundation.org/APEX.htm

This company is dedicated to bringing forth awareness of new sources of energy technologies and to do planetary explorations. That is where we formed the second company for profit called Advanced Planetary Explorations, LLC. This company owns the film rights, the copyrights and trademarks for the Inner Earth Expedition.

There is a new DVD documentary we produced called ***The Inner Earth Expedi-***

tion Part One. It is filmed on location at Mount Shasta and in Tibet. There is remarkable footage never before seen in the West that proves beyond any doubt that the idea that the Earth is hollow has roots in ancient history. Couple that with the idea that ancient man has inextricably recorded his involvement with off-world beings, and you have a factor of this story that is simply stunning.

There are three books we have written, and one with which we are participating in a reissue. The ***Ark of Millions of Years*** has three volumes. They cover the creation and destiny of the Earth, the year 2012 mysteries, and a final book called ***Unlocking the Secret.*** These are all for sale at all bookstores and Amazon and Barnes & Noble as well as through our website at: www.arkofmillionsofyears.com

The Elder Ones from the Inner Earth

By Brad Steiger

In Pershing County, Nevada, a shoe print was found in Triassic limestone, strata indicative of 400 million years, in which the fossilized evidence clearly revealed finely wrought double-stitching in the seams.

Early in 1975 Dr. Stanley Rhine of the University of New Mexico announced his discovery of humanlike footprints in strata indicative of 40 million years old.

Fossilized tracks of both bare and shod feet of decidedly humanlike impression have been found in rocks from the Carboniferous to the Cambrian period in geological sites ranging from Virginia and Pennsylvania, through Kentucky, Illinois, Missouri, Utah, Oklahoma, and Texas. The prints give every evidence of having been made by some unknown bipedal creatures with humanlike feet about 250 to 500 million years ago.

According to conventional science, we humans, *Homo sapiens,* are officially less than 150,000 years old, and we became the dominant species roughly 45,000 years ago. We will leave the scientists to engage in their sometimes heated debate over exactly when the genus *Homo* replaced the apelike *Australopithecus*. The mystery on which we shall focus our attention is this: If our species' oldest ancestor is but 3.18 million years old, and the triumphant exodus of our evolving species out of Africa took place only around 150,000 years ago, then how could these geologic strata throughout the United States and scattered around the world be revealing so many "human" footprints, tools, and other artifacts roughly 250-500-million years old?

In 1953, miners of the Lion coal mine of Wattis, Utah, broke into a network of tunnels between five and six feet in height and width, which contained piles of coal of such vast antiquity that it had become weathered to a state of uselessness for any kind of burning or heat. A search outside the mountain in direct line with the tunnels revealed no sign of any entrance. Since the tunnels were discovered when the miners were working an eight-foot coal seam at 8,500 feet, the evidence is irrefutable that an undetermined someone had conducted an extremely ambitious mining project so far back in time that all exterior traces had been eroded away.

According to Professor John E. Wilson of the Department of Engineering, University of Utah, the tunnels "without a doubt" were man-made: "Though no evidence was found at the outcrop, the tunnels apparently were driven some 450 feet from the outside to the point where the present workings broke into them...There is no visible basis for dating the tunnels...."(February 1954 issue of *Coal Age)*

Jesse D. Jennings, professor of anthropology at the University of Utah, could offer no opinion as to the identity of the mysterious ancient miners, but he denied that such vast tunnels and coal mining rooms could have been the work of any Native American tribes.

In addition to deep-driven tunnels with coal so ancient that it is no longer able to burn, there are an incredible number of unexplained finds in mines that indicate some intelligent workers who thrived in those epochs we consider prehistoric. To list only a very few, I will mention the following:

A strange, imprinted slab was found in a coal mine. The artifact was decorated with diamond-shaped squares with the face of an old man in each box.

In another coal mine discovery, miners found smooth, polished concrete blocks which formed a solid wall. According to one miner's testimony, he chipped one block open only to discover the standard mixture of sand and cement that makes up most typical building blocks of today.

An iron spike was discovered in a silver mine in Peru.

An iron implement was found in a Scottish coalbed, estimated to be millions of years older than humans are believed to have existed.

A metal, bell-shaped vessel, inlaid with a silver floral design, was blasted out of solid rock near Dorchester, Massachusetts.

In 1912, two employees of the Municipal Electric Plant, Thomas, Oklahoma, used a sledge to break open a chunk of coal too large for the furnace. An iron pot toppled from the center of the chunk, leaving an impression in the coal.

Carved bones, chalk, stones, together with what would appear to be greatly ornamented coins have been brought up from great depths during well-drilling operations.

Two hypotheses come immediately to mind which may explain the presence of such perplexing evidence of a human or humanoid presence in a vast antiquity: 1.] such artifacts as those listed above were manufactured by an advanced civilization on Earth which, due either to natural or technological catastrophe, was destroyed and their survivors retreated to build an underground place of refuge; 2.] they are vestiges of a highly technological civilization of extraterrestrial origin, which visited this planet millions of years ago, leaving behind colonists who retreated beneath the Earth's surface, but who still maintain contact with their home planet.

Alfred Scadding was one of two survivors of the famous 1936 Moose River Mine disaster in Nova Scotia. Just minutes before the mines caved in, he was on his way to join other workers. But then, as he later told the story:

"I came to a cross cut, a tunnel running across the one I was in, and as I passed I looked left. I saw a small light, like a flashlight, about two feet from the ground and swinging as if in someone's hand, moving away from me. Two minutes after I saw the light, the mine came in on us."

After his rescue, Scadding was told that there were no human beings down in the mine at that time other than the two miners who were trapped with him. Yet he said that after the three of them had been trapped for some time, they clearly heard the sounds of shouting and laughter. Scadding insisted that they were all clear-headed and conscious, and at first they thought they were somehow hearing children playing and that there must be a vent somewhere to the surface. For twenty-four hours, Scadding said, they heard the bizarre sounds of people laughing and shouting and having fun.

Who could find the plight of miners trapped in a cave-in to be the source of amusement? Ray Palmer would quickly have nominated Richard Shaver's dero for such a dubious distinction.

Ray Palmer was fiction editor of the Ziff-Davis stable of magazines from February 1938 to September 1949, in September of 1944 when a letter from a Richard S. Shaver came to his attention. In what at first appeared to be a claim by some crackpot about an ancient language that "should not be lost to the world," Palmer, more or less on a whim, decided to print the letter, complete with specimens of the alleged language, in the next issue of *Amazing Stories.*

The publication of the strange letter brought an avalanche of mail to Palmer's desk. All of the intrigued letters to the editor wanted to know where Shaver had acquired the alphabet displayed in his correspondence. Smelling a good story in the making, Palmer relayed the curiosity of the magazine's readers to Shaver and received a 10,000 word manuscript in reply. Impressed with the sincerity of the crude manuscript, which Shaver had ominously entitled, "A Warning to Future Man," Palmer retitled the piece, "I Remember Lemuria," added a few trimmings and polish, and published it in the March 1945 issue of *Amazing Stories*, thereby setting off what *Life* magazine six years later would declare "the celebrated rumpus that racked the science-fiction world."

Shaver and Palmer had created a "rumpus," because the stories claimed to be true accounts of human interaction with a race of malformed subhuman creatures called "deros" who inhabited a vast system of underground cities all over the world. The ancestors of the dero were a race of people called the Abandondero, descendents of those who were unable to leave the planet when the "Titans" or "Atlans" from Lemuria discovered that the sun's radiations were radioactive and thereby limiting to life. While those who left Earth in a mass exodus sought a planet with an uncontaminated sun, the Abandondero planned to escape the radioactive poisoning by abandoning the surface and creating cities in vast underground caverns.

Although the sun does hasten the aging process, it also has many health-giving rays which the Inner Earth dwellers had then denied themselves. Vast numbers of the underpeople began to degenerate into physically stunted near-idiots, no longer capable of constructive reasoning. According to Richard Shaver, these were the "dero," the detrimental or degenerate robots. "Robot" as Shaver uses the word doesn't mean a mechanical representation of human, but is rather a designation for those who are governed by degenerative, negative forces.

Standing between the viciousness of the degenerate dero and the surface civilization are the "tero" ("T" was the Atlans' symbol of deity in their religion; therefore the "t" in tero represents good). The tero have learned methods of staving off much of the mental degenerative effects of their subterranean way of life by the use of certain machines, chemicals, and beneficial rays. They have not been successful in discovering a means whereby they are able to prevent premature aging, however, and they die at an average age of fifty.

Shaver's "warning" to future humankind is that the dero are becoming more numerous and have scattered the benign tero with their constant attacks. The greatest threat to us lies in the grim fact that the dero have access to all the machines of the Atlan technology, but they don't have the intelligence or the highly developed moral sense of the ancients to use these machines responsibly.

The dero have possession of "vision ray machines" that can penetrate solid rock and pick up scenes all over Earth. In order to accomplish instant transport from one point to another, they have access to the Atlans' teleportation units. Frighteningly, the dero long ago gained control of the mental machinery that can induce "solid" illusions, dreams, and compulsions in topsiders. In addition to the aerial craft that we call UFOs, the dero possess death rays that can wreak terrible havoc.

According to Shaver, the dero are notorious for their sexual orgies, and they apply "stim" machines that revitalize sexual virility and "ben" rays that heal and restore the physical body. These mechanisms were created the ancient Atlans thousands of years ago and are still in perfect working order, due to the high degree of technical perfection with which they were constructed.

We surface dwellers are the descendants of the Abandondero who were unable to gain access to the caves at the time of the great exodus of the Titans from Earth. Most of our early ancestors died off; some degenerated into such lumbering hominids as Neanderthal; others, the hardy ones, survived, and through the centuries our species has developed a greater tolerance for the sun, which allows us to live even longer than the subsurface tero with their machines of rejuvenation. At the same time, the beneficient rays of the sun have prevented in our kind the mental and physical deterioration that perverts the dero and weakens the tero.

Although we have a common heritage with the tero and the dero, the passage of time has prevented the great mass of surface dwellers from possessing more than dim memories of the glory days of Atlantis, Lemuria, Mu, and the epochs when there were "giants in the Earth." However, Shaver cautions us, by no means have the dero forgotten us. These sadistic monsters take enormous delight in creating terrible accidents, confusing the goals of our political leaders, provoking surface wars between nations, and even in causing nightmares by focusing "dream mech" on us while we sleep.

In November 1997, twenty-two-year-old Duane Berger told me that he and his friend

Mark, 20, had decided to camp near an old deserted copper mine and soak up some of Arizona's pioneer history. That afternoon, they took a lot of pictures both in and out of the tunnel, and they walked into the mine as far as they felt it was safe to do so.

Later, as daylight was fading, they built a campfire and fixed some steaks, beans, and Texas toast. "By the time it was dark, we had each downed a couple of long-necked beers, and were just sitting around the fire, feeling pretty good about life in general, when we began to hear these terrible screams that seemed to be coming from the old mine."

At first, neither of them knew what to say or how to respond. "Just imagine that you and a buddy are alone out in the desert hills, that as far as you know there is no one else around for miles and miles around, and then, suddenly, you start hearing these godawful female screams coming from an old, deserted mine," Duane asked rhetorically, "what would you do? I think both of us just tried to ignore those pitiful screams for as long as we could."

"So what is that?" Mark finally asked, carefully placing the longneck he had just opened back in the cooler. "And where is it coming from?"

According to Duane's report of the incident, prior to that time the two friends had never really discussed the supernatural or the possible existence of ghosts or creatures of the dark. "But I don't think either of us thought for a moment that those screams could somehow be the product of spirits," Duane said. "The cries and moans sounded just too real, like a whole bunch of women were being tortured or something."

After a few moments of nervous discussion and assessment of the very eerie situation, the two young men were forced to conclude that the screams were definitely coming from somewhere within the mine. They knew that no one other than they had been in the vicinity all that day and there had been no signs of human visitation immediately prior to their arrival that they could discern. "There were no fresh tire tracks or evidence of campfires to indicate that anyone other than the two of us had visited the old mine for a long, long time," Duane said. "We hadn't gone very far into the mine during our exploration, so the only theory we could devise is that someone was living deeper within the mine and that someone—whoever it might be—was terribly mistreating whatever women were with them."

Although neither of them had ever visualized himself as a hero, neither could they imagine that they could remain detached from a scene in which women might be being held and tortured by some cruel captors. "The only weapons we had were the steak knives and a tire iron," Duane said, "but we knew that we couldn't just sit there and listen to those poor women being so horribly mistreated."

The two friends mustered their courage and entered the mine shaft. "We had barely walked a dozen yards when we saw a greenish glow ahead of us," Duane stated. "As we got closer, we could make out the dark figures of two men in hooded robes. It was clear that they intended to block our going any farther into the mine."

As soon as they saw the two hooded figures, Duane and Mark were convinced that they had stumbled upon a cult of some sort that might even be practicing human sacrifice. "We whispered to each other that we had really done it now," Duane said. "Now the cultists would probably come after us to keep us from telling the authorities about their satanic practices in the old mine."

But as the frightened young men drew nearer to the light, they saw that their adversaries were barely five feet in height. With growing confidence that the two of them—both muscular men over six feet tall— could physically defend themselves against a bunch of "midget cultists," Duane and Mark boldly demanded that the hooded figures release the women they were hurting.

That was when a deep, mechanical voice boomed out of the cowled figures in unison and told them: *"The women are beyond your help! Leave at once or perish! Leave at once—or you shall join them in the caves."*

Duane put the beam of his flashlight beam directly into the face of one of their robed opponents, and he was astonished to see what appeared to be some kind of red harlequin-type mask covering the being's upper facial features. "The rest of his face seemed to be a really sickly gray color," Duane said. "He didn't appreciate the light in his eyes, and he yelled what I assumed was a curse in some strange language."

Next, complains Duane, "comes the part that no one ever believes." The robed figures produced some type of wandlike instrument and directed a yellow light at the two young men that held them both immobile. Next, they aimed a greenish beam against a wall of the mine shaft. The wall of solid rock seemed to melt away, allowing them to walk into the wall and disappear. Within seconds, the wall was once again nothing but hard rock.

Duane said that the effects of the yellow light dissipated in less than a minute, leaving their bodies feeling "tingling, like the sensation you get when you bump your 'crazy bone' in your elbow."

After the effects of the ray had worn off, Duane and Mark spent no more than ten or twelve seconds deciding what they should do next. "We realized that we were up against something and *someone* totally beyond our experience, our imagination. We knew that we had encountered some incredible supernatural beings or aliens from another world or demons from hell—so we just kicked out the campfire, grabbed up our gear, and got the hell out of there as fast as we could possibly move."

In the years since their frightening encounter with the mysterious cave beings, Duane said that he often reflects on the fate of the women that they heard screaming from within the mine. "I know that there was nothing that we could have done to help them," he said. "A couple of steak knives couldn't compare to rayguns that could momentarily paralyze you, then open and close holes in stone walls. Some nights when I can hear those awful screams again in my mind, it seems to me as though we were hearing tormented souls crying out regard, for the ancient text frequently describes Rama as an emissary from *Agharta,* who arrived among the people on an aerial vehicle. It is remarkable to note that the *Ramayana* contains a description of a "flying saucer" as detailed as any provided by contemporary UFO contactees.

One constant that might be said about the Old Ones from underground is their everlasting quest for new blood from us topsiders, often times attempting to seduce our adult men and women or kidnapping our infants from their cribs and our children from the city streets and forest lanes. In this regard, they are very much like the fairy folk. And in fact, they might have given rise to the fairy legends—or vice versa. On the other hand, what appear to be fairies or Old Ones might be, in reality, demonic entities manifesting from some other dimension with an aggressive agenda of seduction, deceit, and destruction. As those who embark upon a serious study of those entities from out of the dark who seek to molest humankind in various and sundry ways, there may well be a great deal of overlapping among the kinds of categories into which we with our finite human minds attempt to place these shadowy manifestations. In the final analysis, we may only be dealing with the forces of good and evil and viewing them through their reflections in the myriad mirrors of human consciousness.

****

The Hollow Earth Hassle
Of Mary Jane Martin
And The Incredible Story
Of Richard Shaver
By Sean Casteel

For "technical purposes," Mary Jane Martin is the editor of the ***"The Best Of The Hollow Hassle."*** The material in this publication is composed of letters and published articles that were used in the "Hollow Hassle" newsletter that Mary Jane put out for several years. She knew everyone in the Shaver-Hollow Earth field, a field that was small and limited due to its frankly bizarre nature. The Shaver Mystery is an offshoot of the Hollow Earth theory; it differs in that its chief promoter, Richard Shaver, said the world wasn't necessarily hollow, but that it housed a series of vast underground cities that were connected by tunnels that circled the inside of the globe. This tunnel system was originally constructed by ancient inhabitants of Earth who fled from the radioactive surface to build a new home underground. Today, all manner of denizens inhabit the inner earth.

Mary is the last of the Richard Shaver "inner circle." We felt it important that we work with her in putting this material together into a practical framework so that it might be available to other students of these remarkable subjects.

Of the original participants in the drama that came to be known as the Shaver Mysteries, very few remain alive today. Both Richard Shaver and his mentor, Raymond Palmer, passed away in 1975, each of them steadfastly maintaining that the work they had published about the Tero and Dero of the Hollow Earth was factual, though its heyday with diehard believers had long since passed.

Among the handful of believers who have kept the subject of the Shaver Mysteries alive and "out there," it was left to Mary Jane to begin publishing a newsletter in the early 1970s devoted to the latest findings about the dark kingdom below our feet that sends such endless misery to us hapless mortals on the surface.

In an interview conducted for this book, we spoke to Mary Jane and asked how she first came to the subject. She said it all started when she saw an ad for *"The Smoky God, Or A Voyage To The Inner World,"* a 1908 novel by Willis George Emerson which is presented as a true account of a Norwegian sailor who sailed through an entrance to the Earth's interior at the North Pole.

"I can't recall what the ad said," Mary Jane said, "or what piqued my interest enough to send for it, but I have never regretted that I did. This was my first encounter with the theory of a Hollow Earth. I was also receiving a newsletter put out by Dorothy Starr, with its main interest being in the possibility of a polar shift. I wrote to Dorothy and asked her if any of her readers were interested in the theory of a Hollow Earth. She had one member who shared my interest, namely Tom LeVesque, who I started to correspond with."

It was around that time that Mary Jane began printing her own small newsletter called "The Hollow Hassle." LeVesque became her coeditor, and the newsletter was published monthly for a total of thirteen issues. Mary Jane and LeVesque were married in 1973, and began to travel around the country investigating paranormal phenomena, including cattle mutilations.

Mary Jane said that in the wake of reading *"The Smoky God"* and another book called *"Etidorhpa"* (an 1898 novel by John Uri Lloyd about a Freemason who descends to the Inner Earth through a cave in Kentucky and encounters strange forms of life there), she knew that solid, real-world information to back up the claims of Shaver and others would be hard to come by.

"I knew that it would be a 'hassle' to find any information on this," she explained, "thus the title 'The Hollow Hassle.'"

Due to their travel schedule and dwindling funds, publication of the newsletter ceased for a time. After she and LeVesque separated in 1981, Mary Jane began to print the newsletter again as a quarterly, running for about another seventeen issues into the mid-1980s.

It was a gut feeling about Richard Shaver's writings that kept her believing for so long.

"There was a lot of factual evidence to show that a Hollow Earth had a good possibility of being true," she said. "Many people are more versed in the scientific aspects than I am, but you do have things like the Narwhales that travel north and disappear. Many legends talk of their ancestors disappearing further north, possibly entering through the North Pole entrance, just as the Narwhales probably are."

Along the way, Mary Jane struck up a relationship with Shaver himself.

"Initially," she said, "I started to correspond [by regular mail] with Dick Shaver, but I did go to his Arkansas home twice. The first time, he looked healthy, but the second visit Dick looked thinner and worn down. I also did a radio talk show interview with Dick, on the Hilly Rose Show. Tom and I did the first show by ourselves, and on the next show, Dick came in at about the half-way mark."

Mary Jane also came to know others who were likewise in pursuit of the truth about the Shaver Mysteries.

"I was very fortunate to be in touch with a number of very interesting people," she said. "They included Richard Toronto, of Shaverton fame, Charles Marcoux, who died on the way to Blowing Cave in Arkansas, Joan O'Connell from *'The New Atlantean Journal,'* and Bruce Walton, now known as 'Branton,' who was an excellent researcher on the Hollow Earth/Inner Earth."

Did Mary Jane ever do any exploring of caves herself?

"I have explored some caves," she replied, "and I also went to a number of tourist caves. Unfortunately, I did not find a tunnel that led to the Inner Earth, but many of the tourist caves have areas where you are not allowed to go, so who knows how far those areas go? I do feel that the Mammoth Cave in Kentucky may be an entrance."

That there is something wicked lurking in the hollow places is accepted without question by Mary Jane.

"I do believe there is evil in those caves," she said, "and Richard Shaver warned us not to go into the caves. There are too many crazy things that happen on Earth, with no apparent reason for them to happen. One man got hit by lightning twice in his life. What are the odds of that? Young people do things that are very evil and they seem to have no control over their actions. Deros would explain a lot of things. Also, when Ray Palmer stayed overnight at Richard's house, he heard voices."

Still, a certain amount of controversy continues to enshroud the relationship of Shaver and Palmer and the literal truth as understood between them. For example,

Palmer once declared that during the time Shaver was allegedly underground, Shaver was instead in a mental institution in a coma. We asked Mary Jane for her thoughts on the controversy.

"That's a tough question," she said. "A lot of people think it was an astral trip that Richard took while being in a coma, and that may be. But whether it's an actual trip or an astral one, on some level it is real. It certainly was to Richard, and I'm inclined to believe him. We got pretty close in the years that we knew each other.

"I feel that Richard wrote what he believed to be true," Mary Jane continued, "and then Palmer dressed it up to make it more exciting and saleable. Palmer only paid Richard one and a half cents per word, and I think there was trouble about that."

Much of the unhappy events that have transpired in the years since Mary Jane blames quite firmly on the Dero, including her own health problems, among other things.

"At one time," she said, "I do think they

were stopping me from putting out *'The Hollow Hassle,'* as I had been rushed to the hospital twice with chest pains. It wasn't just me that was being hit by the Deros. Joan O'Connell, who had published more Hollow Earth info, died from a heart attack. She had no heart problems previously. Then her material went to Gray Barker, who was going to continue publishing her newsletter. He died three months after Joan, from a heart attack, I believe. Then Charles Marcoux was killed by a number of bees as he was heading towards Blowing Cave in Arkansas."

But nothing tops the death of Richard Shaver himself when it comes to strange factors being at play.

"Richard Shaver's death was highly suspect also," Mary Jane said. "He had signed a contract to come to Hollywood and be a consultant on a movie about the Teros and Deros. He was very excited and even got new dentures for the occasion. Then he came down with locked bowels and had to go into the hospital. He told his wife Dot that the Deros would not let him make this movie and he would die in the hospital. She assured him that it was not a serious operation and that he would be fine."

Dot was quite correct that the surgery itself would go well. But as he lay recovering in his hospital bed, Shaver suffered a pair of small heart attacks.

"Neither of which should have killed him," Mary Jane said, "but he died in that hospital. His prediction came true. The Deros would not let him live to make that movie. Afterwards, Dot could not find the contract for the movie or who was making it, as we wanted to check into that further."

Finally, Mary Jane said the Hollow Earth may have been created initially as the Garden of Eden, despite the scoffing of modern day science.

"Science is wrong a lot," she said, "and they still don't really know much about what is below our feet. Someone told me that if God was going to build a house for Adam and Eve, would he build it so they had to live on the porch outside the house, or would he build it where there was no glaring sun, with large gardens of fruit, stable temperatures, etc., such as the Hollow Earth? Perhaps when Adam and Eve got thrown out of the Garden, it meant that they were tossed out of the Inner World, to suffer the extreme climates on the outside of the Earth."

Were we indeed cast out of an Inner Earth paradise when we fell from grace? Like so much of the Shaver Mysteries to which Mary Jane has devoted years of study, the answer may lie in some hidden place that only Richard Shaver and a few others have ever reached. In any case, we are left to struggle against the Dero ourselves, or whatever the embodiment of evil that still tortures mankind is ultimately called. And Mary Jane's place in that overall scheme of things can be read right here, in the pages of yet another attempt to make sense of the unknowable before it is too late to make sense of anything.

Exploring The "Hidden World" Series Of Richard Shaver: Giving Evil A New Name

For those who find Shaver's concept of

a "Hollow Earth" interesting, perhaps a bit of background on the man himself would be in order to round out our efforts to show how he became an important piece of the overall subterranean world "lifestyle."

The incredible story of Richard Shaver and his underground race of demonic fiends, creatures he claimed live deep below us and are said to have hijacked wonderful inventions like UFOs from alien visitors eons ago, has almost never been completely told. But thanks to researchers and publishers like Timothy Green Beckley, who believes that not every strange object seen in the sky has to be from outer space, an entire series of books has been saved from obscurity after a half century in oblivion and has once again been brought into the light of day.

"The Hidden World," volumes one through six, are part of a set of sixteen original books that were first published in the 1960s and have become rare collector's items since that time, often selling for as much as $80 per volume through rare book dealers. The books – all around 200 pages long, with colorful covers and printed in large format editions – detail a vast underground world hidden from view and known only to a handful of surface dwellers, mortals who are thought to be utterly mad because they claim to hear voices being projected at them by the ancient "telog" machines operated by the "dero."

And who are the dero? To find that answer, one must go back nearly seventy years to a moment when, by some otherworldly form of literary grace, Richard Shaver's sloppily typed manuscript was rescued from total oblivion by an editor with acute hearing who was somehow fated to bring to light a mystery that still thrives among some Inner Earth enthusiasts even now in the 21st century.

The story goes like this: It was December of 1943. A man named Ray Palmer was an editor for a magazine publishing house called Ziff-Davis and in charge of several pulp magazines. One day at work, he heard another editor drop a letter in his trashcan with the words, "The world is sure full of crackpots!" Palmer was to write later that he could hear the other editor's contemptuous remark through the wall between their offices and that he decided to look at the letter himself.

The letter contained a key to understanding an ancient language called Mantong, said to be the father tongue of all human languages on earth. After experimenting a little with some of the claims made about the alphabet of Mantong, and being surprised to see that the letter writer's theories were indeed correct, even when working with languages other than English, Palmer decided to publish the letter.

"The results made publishing history," Palmer later wrote, "insofar as pulp magazines were concerned. Many hundreds of letters poured in, and the net result was a letter to Richard S. Shaver asking him where he got his alphabet. The answer was in the form of a 10,000 word manuscript, typed with what was certainly the ultimate non-ability at the typewriter, and entitled 'A Warning To Future Man.'"

Palmer read Shaver's manuscript and

marveled that Shaver was making no attempt to "sell" his work but instead seemed to be operating out of a sincere desire to warn mankind about the underground race Shaver called "the dero." Dero was a combination of the words "degenerate" and "robot," and those wicked dwellers inside the earth were to be described in exacting detail by Shaver for many years to come.

Palmer took Shaver's lengthy letter and used it as the basis for a 31,000 word article called *"I Remember Lemuria!"* and published it in the magazine ***"Amazing Stories."*** Palmer continued to publish Shaver's work for many years, often to the dismay of his magazine's loyal readership, who expected to read the latest pulp science fiction stories, not an allegedly nonfiction piece that seemed to be the ravings of a semi-literate lunatic.

But there were also those readers who took Shaver's account very much to heart, and the magazines bearing Shaver's stories on the cover sold phenomenally well, to the extent that the magazine exhausted its wartime ration of pulp paper and could not print enough copies to meet the demand.

It is that element of the reading public who responded so enthusiastically to Shaver's claims that concerns us here. Shaver had tapped into something, a way of viewing the world and its inherent evil, that struck a chord deep inside many thousands of people who could relate to his story, no matter how bizarre, as being within the realm of their own experience.

And just what was Shaver's story? What had happened to him that in the telling moved so many people to say they'd been there as well? As Shaver himself relates it in an early chapter of *"The Hidden World, Number One,"* he was working on an automobile assembly line in Detroit using a spot welder in the early 1940s when he began to hear voices that seemed to be emanating from his welding tool. At first he thought it was a fellow worker nearby, but he soon realized he was hearing something decidedly more telepathic, the inner thoughts of the men who toiled beside him. From there, he began to hear the voices of people being tormented, screaming in agony and begging for mercy – like the sounds of hell itself.

His next move was to try to flee the voices. He left his home in Detroit and traveled elsewhere, but the voices followed him wherever he went. He came to understand that the voices were being projected from an underground world and that the voices knew he was listening and were planning his destruction. Admittedly it all sounds like the typical delusions of a paranoid schizophrenic, but when you factor in the story's popularity with readers, you are forced to take another look at it from a more sympathetic angle.

Most people, while they are understandably hesitant to admit it, would likely agree that they have at some time suffered the oppression of evil forces one might compare to Shaver's "dero." No one, it seems, has been exempted from a kind of mistreatment that appears somehow to come from another part of existence we cannot define and certainly cannot control. People's personal demons usually seem real enough to them, but talking about them openly is rarely done in polite company. Shaver crossed that line, risking ridicule and public shame, and surprisingly received a resounding response from fellow sufferers who knew exactly where he was coming from.

The monsters called the dero were the completely insane remnant of a race that had existed before mankind on earth. The rays of the sun began to pour down harmful radiation, so some of the earlier race escaped in ships while the less fortunate among them were forced to go underground and live in a system of caves that had existed since the beginning of time.

The dero retreated too late to spare themselves from the madness caused by the poisonous rays of the sun, but they did manage to take with them many of the super-advanced machines their race had developed. With these machines they were able to cause evil and madness on the surface where mankind had come to dwell. They could force hapless humans to do unspeakably wicked things to their fellow man. The dero also possessed a form of technology called "Stem" that could induce deviant sexual feelings in surface dwellers and lead them to acts of perversion and rape. Mankind had always had its own capacity to sin, but the dero caused that evil to rise to monstrous extremes.

This was what Shaver was laboring so hard to warn mankind about, to alert them to the very real presence of an egregious enemy lurking beneath their feet. He would spend the rest of his life in this effort, writing many thousands of words to further elaborate on his claims. As mentioned earlier, Timothy Beckley, the publisher of the ***"Hidden World"*** series, has gathered together a huge portion of the writings of Shaver and his mentor Ray Palmer into a sixteen-volume set, of which the first six volumes are currently available. When it is completed, it will be the most thorough document of what has come to be called the Shaver Mysteries ever compiled.

Volume One includes Ray Palmer's first-hand account of how he discovered Shaver's initial letter and made the momentous decision to actually publish it. Palmer also recounts visiting Shaver and his wife in their home; Palmer actually heard a few mysterious voices himself during his stay there. One can also read Shaver's account of how he first began to hear the voices of the dero in his own words. The complete text of *"I Remember Lemuria!"* is also included in Volume One, so that the reader can experience firsthand the story that launched Shaver into the pulp magazine stratosphere.

About his reading public, Shaver writes, "To me, struggling to find an opening out of the morass (no longer just for myself, but now for all mankind), the flood of letters I received from other sufferers was a crushing blow, bringing hopeless despair. The caverns were not, I realized now, a localized thing – they extended underneath every area of the earth. The evidence of their activity and strength piled up, until I could not help but conclude that there is no answer for present day man. He cannot break their power over him, nor remedy the ills they visit upon him."

Shaver also writes in a similar pessimistic way about the UFOs, which first received worldwide attention with Kenneth Arnold's sighting in 1947, a few brief years after the publication of *"I Remember Lemuria!"*

"The visits of the saucers bring with them, for me, fresh despair. For I see them as proof of the caverns' contact with space. Knowing the cave people, I know that if any of the visiting saucers were benevolent visitors bringing gifts and scientific knowledge to the surface people, they would be destroyed. To me, that explains the failure to contact our surface government, because those saucers that are not destroyed are our ancient enemies."

What Shaver is talking about is something similar to a concept first put forth by alien abduction researcher Budd Hopkins. Hopkins coined the phrase "confirmation anxiety" to describe what happens when an abductee finds proof of the reality of his experiences, such as seeing a mark left behind on his body after recalling that a skin sample has been taken during an abduction episode. A person needs to have some part of his mind in a state of doubt to function as a hiding place where he can call what he has experienced unreal. Since an abductee is often in a dreamlike state while the experience is happening, he has the luxury of filing the experience away in the "unknown basket" and maintaining a more normal connection with everyday reality. When something happens to drive the troublesome memory into a place where the abductee cannot deny that something frightening and strange has really happened to him after all, when his dreams are "confirmed" for him, a whole new kind of anxiety kicks in.

For Shaver, the mass outpouring of letters his writings received and the coming of the flying saucers a few years after his story was made public were not a consolation or a vindication but rather an unimpeachable testimony to the reality of his tormenting voices. He suffered despair on a whole new level, because now there really was nowhere to run, no way to deny the widespread nature of a phenomenon he half-hoped was a misfortune limited to just himself alone.

But of course there remains an audience eager to know about the mysteries that so burdened Shaver. Timothy Beckley of Global Communications has made a sort of cottage industry out of interest in the Inner and Hollow Earth theories, saving some old and rare books from obscurity and publishing up-to-date compendiums written by more recent researchers. His most popular titles dealing with this subject include: *"Twilight, Hidden Chambers Beneath The Earth,"* by T. Lobsang Rampa; *"Underground Alien Bio Lab At Dulce: The Bennewitz UFO Papers"*; *"Admiral Byrd's Secret Journey Beyond The Poles,"* by Tim Swartz; *"Reality Of The Serpent Race And The Subterranean Origin Of UFOs,"* by Branton; *"Best Of The Hollow Earth Hassle,"* by Mary J. Martin; and *"Finding Lost Atlantis Inside The Hollow Earth,"* by the late British writer Brinsely Le Poer Trench, the Earl of Clancarty.

And so it is left to us, decades after the deaths of Shaver and Palmer, to try to pick up the pieces and understand Shaver's torture in ways that can help us to deal with the very vocal evils of our own time. And

Global Communications' ambitious reprinting of the complete writings of Richard Shaver can help us in that endeavor, one volume at a time.

[To read more by Sean Casteel, visit his website at www.seancasteel.com]

Danish artist Max Fyfield shows subsurface layers and the wide range of beings who inhabit the inner Earth.

Printed in Great Britain
by Amazon

36948109R00205